Books
for
Early Childhood

Books
for
Early Childhood

A Developmental Perspective

Compiled by
Jean A. Pardeck
and
John T. Pardeck

Bibliographies and Indexes in Psychology, Number 3

GREENWOOD PRESS
New York • Westport, Connecticut • London

LIBRARY OF CONGRESS CATALOGING-IN-PUBLICATION DATA

Pardeck, Jean A.
  Books for early childhood.

  (Bibliographies and indexes in psychology,
ISSN 0742-681X ; no. 3)
    Includes indexes.
    1. Bibliotherapy for children. 2. Child development—
Juvenile literature—Abstracts. 3. Child development—
Juvenile literature—Bibliography. 4. Children's
literature—Abstracts. 5. Children's literature—
Bibliography. 6. Children—Books and reading.
I. Pardeck, John T. II. Title. III. Series.
RJ505.B5P36 1986   155.4'13   86-14989
ISBN 0-313-24576-2 (lib. bdg. : alk. paper)

Library of Congress Catalog Card Number: 86-14989
ISBN: 0-313-24576-2
ISSN: 0742-681X

First published in 1986

Greenwood Press, Inc.
88 Post Road West, Westport, Connecticut 06881

Printed in the United States of America

∞™

The paper used in this book complies with the
Permanent Paper Standard issued by the National
Information Standards Organization (Z39.48-1984).

10 9 8 7 6 5 4 3 2 1

To James Kenneth Pardeck and Jonathan Travis Pardeck
our developmental specialists

Contents

Preface

Purpose

Purpose

The primary purpose of this book is to provide counselors, social workers, psychiatrists, teachers, and other helping professionals with readily available information on children's literature that can help preschoolers deal with the developmental process. This book can also be used by those who may not be trained in child development, such as librarians and parents.

The book is based on the bibliotherapeutic approach, an emerging helping strategy that can be used not only for clinical problems, but also as focused on in this book, as a technique for helping children handle developmental needs. By recognizing bibliotherapy as a tool that can be used in this fashion, its usefulness extends not only to those trained in child development as a specialization, but also to those not necessarily trained in the child development field.

For those who do not have a background in bibliotherapy, an introduction to this emerging field is presented in Chapter 1. Also focused on in Chapter 1 is a review of the major theories of child development and a discussion of the ways that literature can be used to help preschool children cope with developmental growth. It is emphasized that, regardless of which developmental perspective one takes, literature can be a useful tool for helping children deal with physical, social, and emotional development. Nine different topics have been identified by the authors as important areas of early child development. These topics are anger and other emotions, attitudes and values, family relationships, fear and fantasy, motor development and physical change, peers and school, self-image and sex roles, single-parent and blended families, and special developmental needs. There are 347 children's books annotated in this work, illustrating all of these important areas of child development.

Coverage and Scope

The books annotated in this work were published between 1980

and 1985. The general criteria established for a book to be annotated were
(1) the book had to be a children's literary work that related to one or more of the nine developmental areas; and
(2) the book had to have either a character of preschool age or an animal character with human qualities.

As the focus of this work was on locating children's books dealing with physical, social, or emotional development, the literary merit of individual books was not a consideration. Rather than judge each book in terms of plot development, the quality of illustrations, and so on, the authors simply chose those children's books that realistically portray a developmental stage or task.

There are ten chapters in this work, beginning with an introductory chapter that is followed by nine chapters covering children's books on developmental needs. Each of the chapters covering a developmental area includes a synopsis in order to acquaint the reader with a particular developmental issue. Those synopses are not meant to be inclusive of all that is known about a particular area of development; rather they provide an overview of an area of development as it relates to the preschool child. Also included in the synopsis is a discussion of that particular developmental need as found in early childhood literature and a presentation of techniques that the helping person can utilize to prompt discussion and other responses to the literature from the child.

Entries

The annotated entries for the books in this work are arranged within each chapter in alphabetical order by the author's last name. Many of the books listed in a particular chapter that deal with more than one developmental area are cross-referenced in other chapters. Each entry provides a bibliographic citation, followed by a synopsis of the book and the age level for which the book is most useful, ranging from two to six years. Each bibliographic citation includes the author, title of the book, place of publication, name of publisher, date of publication, and number of pages in the book. The synopsis of each book annotated generally mentions the gender of the book's main character. Other important characters within the book are presented as they relate to the main character. The areas of development that are a part of the book's theme are stressed in the synopsis.

The book synopsis is followed by an interest level (IL). This interest level was determined by the book format and by the developmental area(s) stressed in the book. Interest levels fall into the categories of two to four years, four to six years, and the inclusive category of two to six years. This inclusive category was used because certain books were felt to be appropriate for children at every stage of the early childhood continuum. Other books, due to the abundance or lack of illustrations or because of sentence length, were felt to be better suited to the younger preschool child aged two to four or to the older preschool child aged four to six. The developmental area stressed in the book also determined the interest level category; for example, a book about toilet training would be of most use to the younger preschool child, while a book about attending kindergarten would be best for the older preschool child.

Indexes

The Author Index is a guide to the individuals who wrote the books annotated in each chapter. The Title Index helps the reader locate a particular work by title. The numbers following the authors and titles in these two indexes refer to the books' main entry numbers within each of the nine chapters.

The Subject Index serves two functions. It helps the user locate materials about a specific subject that may or may not be one of the nine areas of development (for example, Attitudes, a main developmental area, is a heading within the Subject Index as are headings such as Manners and Sharing). It also allows the reader to identify entries about subjects such as peers that are found in several of the chapters. Like the two other indexes, the Subject Index refers the reader to appropriate entry numbers within each chapter.

Acknowledgments

The authors would like to thank the staff of the Dean B. Ellis Library, Arkansas State University, for its help in locating children's literature for this work. Margaret Denny alerted the authors to new selections dealing with early childhood coming into the library. Margarett Daniels, Donna Wells, and Terrie Sypolt of the Inter-Library Loan Department were extremely helpful in obtaining books from numerous libraries. Marilyn Umfress gave the authors much assistance in locating reference materials. The authors also thank Mary R. Sive, Editor, Social and Behavioral Sciences, of Greenwood Press for giving us the opportunity to write this book.

1

Introduction

Literature can be used as an effective tool for helping children cope with developmental change. Cionciolo stresses that, "Books can provide a source of psychological relief from the various pressures and concerns that stem from the things that happen to children"(1). In a number of earlier writings, the authors have illustrated how literature can help children cope with both developmental changes and psychological problems(2).

The helping person can use literature as an effective medium to assist children from two years up to six years of age in dealing with developmental change. The use of literature in this manner is known as bibliotherapy. Bibliotherapy, most simply defined, means helping through books. A more detailed definition from the **Dictionary of Education** states that bibliotherapy is the "use of books to influence total development, a process of interaction between the reader and literature which is used for personality assessment, adjustment, growth, clinical and mental hygiene purposes; a concept that ideas inherent in selected reading material can have a therapeutic effect upon the mental or physical ills of the reader"(3). In essence, this detailed definition suggests that bibliotherapy can be used as a treatment technique for not only clinical problems, but also, as stressed in this book, for meeting growth and adjustment needs of children.

Lindeman and Kling also make a very similar conclusion about the uses of bibliotherapy. They emphasize that it can be used as an approach in working with 1) the emotionally troubled, 2) those with minor adjustment problems, and 3) for helping children with developmental needs(4). Clearly, bibliotherapy is a useful tool for helping individuals deal with many different kinds of problems.

History of Using Literature as a Treatment Tool

The uses of literature in helping people cope with problems have been known for centuries. In ancient Thebes, for example, above a library entry was inscribed "The Healing Place of the Soul". The ancient Thebans cherished books for their value as a source for adding to the quality of life. Schrank and Engels have pointed out that the practice of bibliotherapy can be traced back to ancient

Thebes and since then has been used as a source of instruction and healing(5).

In more recent times, several early American schoolbooks such as the **New England Primer** and the **McGuffy Readers** were used with the intent of not only teaching students to read, but also of helping them to develop character and positive values, and to improve personal adjustment(6). Modern educators, including a variety of helping professionals, have come to realize that books can play a positive role in helping people deal with personal adjustment problems.

The development of bibliotherapy as a recognized treatment technique did not really occur until relatively recently. This development is roughly seen as occurring around the turn of the twentieth century. Specifically, two of the first strong advocates for bibliotherapy as a treatment tool were Doctors Karl and William Menninger. A large number of articles appeared in the professional literature in the 1940s; these basically examined the psychological validity of this emerging treatment approach(7). During the 1950s some of the seminal thinking on the subject of bibliotherapy was done by Shrodes who examined the state of the art, thus influencing the field greatly from a philosophical point of view. Shrodes's early definition of bibliotherapy as a process of dynamic interaction between the personality of the reader and literature under the guidance of a counselor or skilled helper continues to heavily influence the field(8). However, recently the authors have argued that bibliotherapy does not have to be a process guided only by the skilled helper(9). As pointed out later in this book, bibliotherapy can be used as a helping technique by those who do not necessarily have clinical training.

In the 1960s, Hannigan and Henderson did extensive on-site research on the impact of bibliotherapy on young drug abusers close to parole. Their research comprises some of the early efforts to test the effectiveness of bibliotherapy as a treatment tool(10). Since the 1960s, at least 24 studies have reported that bibliotherapy can be an effective tool for helping people deal with various emotional and developmental problems(11). Numerous articles have been written in the 1970s and 1980s on bibliotherapy as a useful treatment approach. However, the critics of bibliotherapy continue to be very vocal(12).

Process of Bibliotherapy

An important first step in the bibliotherapeutic process is to match the reader or client with the appropriate literature. Since this book focuses on helping children cope with developmental changes, the literature selected would obviously deal with developmental issues. The child must be able to see similarities between the self and the character in the literature read. An important function of the helping person is to assist the child in seeing these similarities. This stage is referred to as **identification and projection.**

Once identification and projection have occurred, **abreaction and catharsis** is a possibility. This stage is reached when the client has an emotional release that may be expressed verbally or nonverbally. A trained clinician is critical at this level of the bibliotherapeutic process. The final stage of the bibliotherapeutic process is **insight**

and integration; this stage is reached when the client recognizes the self and significant others in the characters within the literature. This information helps the client develop new ways of solving problems.

Obviously, the bibliotherapeutic process is heavily grounded in Freudian psychotherapy. This is evident in the advanced stages of the process, in particular the stage of abreaction and catharsis. However, bibliotherapy also draws on a principle developed in learning theory: Humans learn by imitation. Applied to bibliotherapy, fictional characters become models for positive, adaptive behavior. This is especially helpful for children who lack positive role models in their social environment(13).

The authors have emphasized that bibliotherapy can be useful in helping clients gain insight into problems, providing techniques for relaxation and diversion, creating a medium for the discussion of problems, and helping focus attention outside the self(14).

In this book, the advanced stages of bibliotherapy, abreaction and catharsis, and insight and integration, are not stressed. The focus of this work is on helping children cope with developmental needs, typical problems that do not need advanced therapeutic intervention. Thus the stage of the bibliotherapeutic process which will be referred to by the authors as being helpful for developing preschool children is identification and projection. What this means is that the helping person need not have advanced clinical skills. Applying bibliotherapy mainly at the identification and projection stage can be very useful as an approach for assisting children or clients with minor adjustment problems and in particular, for helping children deal with developmental growth(15).

By focusing on the bibliotherapeutic process at the identification and projection stage, many useful outcomes can occur. Most of these are outcomes that positively impact children who are having problems with developmental needs. These are 1) the child can become psychologically and emotionally involved with characters read about; 2) a child can be taught constructive and positive thinking; 3) reading can encourage free expression concerning the problem; 4) the child can be helped to analyze attitudes and behaviors through reading; 5) reading can help a child to find solutions to a problem; 6) through reading, the child can see similarities between one's own problem and those of others and, finally, 7) literature can help a person accept a problem and offer new and creative ways of dealing with it.

Bibliotherapy can be viewed as a useful means of helping a child cognitively restructure a developmental problem. It is assumed that once children have enough information about a developmental problem, their attitudes and behaviors will change. The story presented in the literature should be discussed with a child thoroughly in order to clear up questions about a problem. There are many creative approaches that can be used to supplement discussions of a book; these will be focused on later in this chapter.

Theories of Development

Within the literature three dominant theories have emerged for explaining human development: 1) the psychoanalytic perspective, 2) the cognitive developmental perspective, and 3) behavioral learning theory. The first two are referred to as stage theories whereas learning theory is a nonstage perspective. The dominant theorist for the psychoanalytic perspective is Sigmund Freud with Jean Piaget being the major theorist for the cognitive developmental orientation. Behavioral learning theory finds its roots in the writings of B.F. Skinner and Albert Bandura. Even though none of the three theories is a complete perspective for explaining the developmental process, each gives a unique contribution toward understanding how children move through the life cycle to adulthood. Although the full spectrum of development will be discussed, this book focuses on the process of development explaining behavior of children from two years up to six years.

The psychoanalytic perspective. Freud stressed in his theory of development that biological forces essentially shape the developmental process. This is basically through the drives resulting from instincts that the human is born with. Freud believed that the human infant is born with a collection of unconscious instinctive drives that supply energy and direction for behavior. Development is seen as the result of changes in the way instinctual energy is organized and channeled. Instinctual energy often changes direction and intensity to insure that balance is maintained in the child. Even when balance is reached, however, instinctual energy continues to fluctuate in the human organism. Consequently, instinctual energy is dynamically organized; it is not static but instead always changing.

Freud's structural model of the personality consists of three major parts: the id, the ego, and the superego. The ego and superego grow from the id as the child develops. As the different parts of the personality develop, the organization of instinctual energy shifts from a loose and uninhibited state to one of structure and control.

At birth the infant is dominated by the instinctual impulses of the id. These impulses operate unconsciously and irrationally. The infant has both physical and psychological needs and is continually forced to find an object that will rapidly satisfy these needs. The search by the infant to satisfy basic physical and psychological needs is referred to as the pleasure principle. As the child grows and matures, new approaches are gradually learned to more realistically satisfy basic needs; this is referred to as the reality principle.

As the child matures, the child gradually develops better mechanisms for reality testing and rational thinking for dealing with the environment; this is referred to as the development of the ego. Much of the ego consists of rational thoughts, perceptions, and plans to help cope with reality. In essence, the child learns to channel instinctual drives in a constructive rational manner.

The final part of the personality to develop is the superego, which consists of moral rules to guide the child's actions. Societal rules are internalized and the dos and don'ts of society are learned and internalized by the child.

Freud theorized that the human organism moves through five distinct stages of development. In terms of the developmental cycle, Freud felt each of the stages had to be properly resolved to insure "normal" development. The first stage of development according to Freud is the **oral** stage. This stage centers on the child's pleasure from stimulation of the oral area--mouth, lips, tongue, and gums. This stage lasts from approximately birth to one year of age.

The period of development lasting from two to three years of age is the **anal** stage. During this stage, the child receives pleasure from elimination activities. This stage is not easily forgotten by parents because it is typically when the child begins to be toilet trained. As the child learns to control elimination with the maturation of the sphincter muscles, the anal stage is at its peak. Even though many disagree with Freud about the actual process that a child goes through during the anal stage, developmental specialists of all persuasions agree that toilet training is a critical time in a child's development(16).

From about four to six years of age, the child moves into the **phallic** stage. During this time period, instinctual energy is focused on the genital area. Physical changes in the child cause this area to be a pleasurable one when stimulated. Freud thought boys and girls become acutely aware of their sexual anatomy and the anatomical differences between the sexes during this stage of development. The awareness of sexual differences sets the stage for a number of complex psychological events referred to as the Oedipus complex in boys and the Electra complex in girls. Each complex involves the child's alternating feelings of love and hate for each parent as the child competes with one parent for love and attention of the other parent. According to Freud, children have a very difficult time working through these complexes, which are actually highly stressful conflicts about sexual affiliation and identity. Even though there is considerable debate about the scientific soundness of the Oedipus and Electra complexes, the curiosity that children develop about sexuality during this stage is clearly evident.

Freud believed that once the Oedipal or Electra complex is resolved, the child enters a period of **latency**. During this stage, from about seven years to thirteen years, no new significant conflicts or impulses are assumed to arise. The primary personality change during this period involves the development of the superego.

The final stage of development occurs from roughly thirteen to nineteen years of age. The child develops a stable sense of personal and sexual identity if the stage is resolved properly. Freud felt that the mature adult emerges out of the **genital** stage of development.

Even though Freud's theory has been criticized extensively by a number of developmental specialists, few would disagree that he identified several critical issues that are an important part of the developmental process. In particular, the toilet training period is extremely stressful for children and parents must approach this period of development with patience and understanding. Children clearly develop an intense curiosity about their sexuality around the ages of four through six. The understanding adult realizes that the curiosity about and exploration of a child's own sexuality is healthy and should be dealt with openly. Freud therefore points out a number of critical issues that appear to be indicative of the early stages of child development.

Cognitive developmental perspective. While the psychoanalytic perspective essentially emphasizes the irrational and unconscious parts of the child, the cognitive approach to development focuses on the child's rational thinking processes. The leading contemporary figure who until his recent death heavily influenced the cognitive developmental perspective was Jean Piaget(17).

Piaget's theory includes four basic stages that the human species moves through: the sensorimotor stage, the preoperational stage, the concrete stage, and the formal operational stage. Piaget's main focus in each of these stages is on the rational and logical thinking of the child moving toward adulthood. Piaget was particularly interested in how intelligence develops from the interplay of hereditary factors and environment. As with psychoanalytic theory, the stages of development are only approximate in terms of the time factor. An individual child may move out of a stage sooner or remain in a stage longer than is indicated by the ages mentioned in the following discussion.

The **sensorimotor** stage lasts from about birth to two years of age. During this stage of development, the infant learns to organize and coordinate sensations and perceptions with physical movement and actions. This coordination is the source of the term sensorimotor. The onset of the stage is when the newborn learns to perform simple tasks such as turning the head, following objects with the eyes, or sucking. The stage ends when the two-year-old develops complex sensoriaction patterns and begins to operate with a primitive symbol system. For example, the child learns to imagine playing with a toy in a certain fashion before actually playing with it. The child also learns simple sentences—for example, "Daddy jump!"—to represent a sensoriaction event that has just occurred.

The second stage the child moves into is the **preoperational** stage which is thought to last from two to seven years of age, cutting across all the early-childhood and a portion of the middle school years. During this time, the child's symbolic system expands greatly and language moves well beyond the capabilities at the end of the sensorimotor stage. Even though a child experiences tremendous intellectual development during this stage, the child's rational thinking processes are still greatly underdeveloped. For example, things tend to be seen from the child's own perspective and no one else's. The child has difficulty manipulating images and representations of events and is therefore likely to get centered in static states and fail to reverse situations intellectually. For example, if liquid is poured from a short container into a tall thin one, the child may notice only that the height of the water changed. If asked to imagine what would happen if the water were returned to the original container, the child would have a difficult time visualizing the reversal—the water going from the tall container into the short one.

The **concrete operational** stage lasts from seven to eleven years of age, including the major portion of the middle school years. During this time, the child's thinking crystallizes into more of a system, and the flaws of the thinking in the earlier stages disappear. In other words, the shift is to a more perfect system of thinking. This shift in thinking is brought about by several changes; one of these is a shift from egocentrism indicative of the preoperational stage to relativism. Relativism is the ability to think from different perspectives and to think simultaneously about two or more aspects of a problem. The child also learns to perform mental tasks such as imagining how to tie a knot or how to shoot a basketball through a hoop. Children in the sensorimotor and preoperational stages are unable to perform these mental operations.

One unique characteristic of the concrete operational stage is that the child has to rely on concrete events in order to think in this way. The child needs to be able to perceive events and objects that are thought about. An interesting aspect of this stage is that the child often fails to distinguish between representation of events and the events themselves because the representations are closely tied to the concrete events. An example of this would be when a child maintains an expectation about what a friend can be expected to do in a certain situation even though the friend seldom does what the child expects. The child treats the expectation as fact rather than as the possibility of a fact.

The final stage of cognitive development is the **formal operational** stage, which emerges between eleven and fourteen years of age. By the time the child has reached this stage, the child has moved into advanced thinking patterns such as the ability to think logically and use abstract propositions. The child is also able to conjure up many hypotheses to account for some event and then test these out in a deductive fashion, just as the scientist does. In essence, the child becomes a rational thinking human being.

For the most part, Piaget's theory has a much wider acceptance than Freud's theory of development. Piaget's theory has guided European and North American scholars for a number of decades. His theory offers a rich description of thought processes and in general a dynamic interpretation of human development. Piaget's preoperational stage is of most concern to this book. What is helpful about understanding the dynamics involved in development during the preoperational stage are the issues related to language development and the intense egocentrism of the child. It must be remembered that the preschool child has problems manipulating images and understanding events; these issues will be clearly reflected in the use of language. Egocentrism, a characteristic extremely indicative of the preoperational stage, is important in the child's learning to cooperate with others including adults and peers. Like Freud, Piaget's theory isolates a number of factors that give much insight into the developmental process.

Behavioral learning theory. The dominant theorist in the area of behavioral learning theory is B.F. Skinner. This perspective is not a stage theory of development, but instead focuses on the impact of the environment on human development and basically suggests that development does not necessarily occur in discrete phases as concluded by the first two theories discussed.

The behavioral learning approach for explaining human behavior and development has not been without controversy(18). Skinner's work in particular has created much discussion because of its philosophical orientation. Skinner basically argues that the nature of human development is best understood by examining behavior of the organism, and not thoughts and feelings of the organism. He believes that looking for internal determinants inhibits the search for the true determinants of behavior, which reside in the external environment of the person. Some theorists claim that Skinner views the organism as an empty shell; however, Skinner has pointed out that he objects to looking for internal determinants of behavior not because they do not exist, but because they are irrelevant to the relationship between stimuli and responses. Stimuli are defined as observable characteristics of the environment that affect the individual and response refers to the overt behavior of the individual. A very simple example of a stimulus would be a child being told to pick up toys; the child actually doing the behavior would be the response.

According to Skinner, one of the major ways stimuli and responses are linked together is through the principle of operant conditioning. Through this process the individual operates on the environment; that is, the individual does something and in turn, something happens to the person. The lives of children and adults are filled with operant conditioning situations. For example, consider the following conversation:

Edward Hey, where did you get the new toy?
Charles My father bought it for me.
Edward Oh yeah, how come?
Charles Because I got mad about something and started crying.
Edward You mean if you cry, your father will buy you a new toy?
Charles I guess that is the way it works(19).

At the center of such occurrences is this principle: Behavior is determined by its consequences. That is, behavior followed by a positive stimulus is likely to occur, while behavior followed by a negative stimulus is not likely to occur. The positive experience is referred to as reinforcement and the negative experience is called punishment.

The principle of operant conditioning has been applied liberally to the term behavior modification. This approach is widely used by counselors, clinicians, teachers and others as a way of resolving problems. Behavior modification experts argue that most emotional problems occur because of their environmental arrangement, meaning that unacceptable behaviors are inadvertently reinforced. Hence the child who participates in delinquent behavior may be doing so because the child is rewarded for such behavior, either through the material rewards of stolen goods or through the peer group. The behavior modification perspective as applied to human development essentially means that the social environment will largely shape the developmental process of the child. Therefore, those who work with children must insure that there is an enriched environment in order for individual children to grow and mature.

Summary. The psychoanalytic perspective and the cognitive developmental perspective are both stage theories; the behavioral learning perspective is a nonstage theory. As pointed out, all three give some insight into the developmental process. The psychoanalytic perspective focuses mainly on subconscious and instinctual forces. The personality is seen as consisting of three major parts—the superego, the ego, and the id. Children pass through a series of psychosexual stages that end in adulthood. The cognitive developmental perspective holds that children move through four stages with the focus being on the development of greater degrees of rational thinking as the child progresses through the developmental process. The behavioral learning theory sees development as the result of learning and adjusting to one's environment. Skinner would largely argue that the human being is basically a product of the environment. The obvious implications of this orientation are that children who have a positive growth environment will develop at an optimum level; those who do not will have developmental deficits.

OVERVIEW OF THE MAJOR
THEORIES OF CHILD DEVELOPMENT

STAGE	APPROXIMATE AGE	FREUD'S PSYCHOSEXUAL STAGES	PIAGET'S COGNITIVE STAGES	BEHAVIORAL LEARNING THEORY
Adolescence	13 to 20 Years	Genital	Formal Operational	* * *
Middle and Late Childhood	6 to 13 Years	Latency	Concrete Operational	* * * *
Early Childhood	2 to 6 Years	Phallic Anal	Preoperational	* * *
Infancy	Birth to 2 Years	Oral	Sensorimotor	*

A comparison of the major theories of child development is illustrated in the table above. This table gives insight into the approximate ages associated with the various stages of the psychoanalytic and cognitive developmental approaches. It should be noted that behavioral learning theory is a nonstage theory and thus is illustrated without reference to any specific stages. As can be seen in the table, the early-childhood period is generally thought to include the age range of two up to six years. According to Freud's psychoanalytic perspective, this would place the preschool child in the anal and phallic psychosexual stages. Although the preoperational stage developed by Piaget goes all the way to age seven, the preschool child would fall within this stage. Children at all ages are impacted by their social environment according to behavioral learning theory. The two- to six-year-old child's environment expands greatly to include peers, perhaps a school experience, and contact with adults other than the parents; therefore, the preschool child moves outside the family system and is greatly impacted by new learning opportunities.

All of these theories contribute to the understanding of the preschool child's development. The developmental needs of these children are reflected in much of the literature available for the preschooler. One of the purposes of bibliotherapy is to meet the developmental needs of children, therefore, an examination of the developmental themes which can be found in early-childhood literature follows.

Developmental Themes in Early
Childhood Literature

There is little doubt that the two stage theories of development, the psychoanalytic perspective and the cognitive developmental perspective, both point to the early-childhood years as being a time of rapid and important change. According to Freud's perspective, the child must move through the anal and phallic stages during the preschool years. Piaget would contend that the preschool child is in the midst of the preoperational stage. Although behavioral learning theory is not a stage theory, its focus on the importance of environment would appear to suggest that the early-childhood years are quite important as well.

Freud's psychoanalytic perspective, with its stress on the development of the personality, views the preschool child as being involved in the stressful anal and phallic stages. Literature dealing with bodily changes and sexual awareness are certainly appropriate for the developing preschool child. In addition, children between the ages of two and six develop coping strategies to deal with their emotions. Therefore, books which explore fears, anger, jealousy, and a variety of other emotions appear to be essential for the preschooler's personality development.

Piaget's developmental scheme places the preschool child in the preoperational stage. At this time, the child is busy discovering the environment through language and intuitive thought. Children in the preoperational stage often explain things that happen by giving life to inanimate objects; for example, if they fall, saying that a toy reached out and tripped them. This delight in humanizing inanimate objects and animals is related to the preschooler's love of fantasy in literature(20). The child's egocentrism during the preschool years must gradually lessen to insure that the child develops socially. Therefore, the developing preschool child has a need to hear stories about relationships developed within the home with parents and siblings, as well as literature dealing with learning to get along with those outside the home, such as teachers and peers.

The emphasis of behavioral learning theory on learning through imitation and role models would indicate that the preschool child may identify with certain characters in the literature. Characters illustrating various attitude and value judgements could be modeled by the preschool child. Books in which parents and other adults serve as positive role models could aid in enhancing the child's sex-role identification and the development of self-image.

Advocates of any of the three theories of development discussed at length earlier would certainly agree that there is a vast difference between the two-year-old and the child who is turning six. During these quite important years, the child experiences great physical change and the increasing ability to perform motor tasks. Early-childhood literature focusing on a child's continuous growth and physical changes such as increase in height and weight would appear to be valuable in helping children understand their physical development. Preschool children can also be aided in coping with their ability to perform increasingly difficult motor tasks, for example, being able to throw a ball rather than just roll it, through the literature available on this topic.

Certain developmental themes in early-childhood literature are of more concern to the two- to four-year-old. Books dealing with dressing skills, play with building blocks and puzzles, or learning to ride a tricycle would all appear to be of interest to this age group. The four- to six-year-old might enjoy books on learning to tie one's shoes, squabbling with friends, or adjusting to kindergarten. Of course, children mature physically, socially, and emotionally at different rates and the individual child's developmental needs, interests, and stage of understanding must always be considered.

Other developmental tasks are faced to a certain extent by children along the whole early-childhood continuum. Early-childhood books are available for the two-year-old, as well as for the five-year-old, who has to contend with a new sibling, a parental divorce, or a day-care experience. Anger, jealousy, and other emotions can be felt by the two-year-old with just as much intensity as the six-year-old, although the coping strategies for each would be different. Very simple picture books focusing on temper tantrums, as well as children's literature on more mature ways of dealing with emotions, are available for the preschooler.

The authors contend that children can respond to and identify with characters in books and that literature can influence development. It appears that writers of children's literature are responding to the needs of children by using developmental tasks as themes for their books. Children's literature in recent years has taken new directions, explored new themes, and opened up possibilities for developing new insights(21). As children grow physically, socially, and emotionally, they find much that is curious and sometimes bewildering in terms of their own and others' behavior. There are many books available that deal with situations and feelings very familiar to young children. When a child is introduced to such books and discovers that the story characters behave in much the same way the child does, the preschool child is thus reassured about problems.

Book selection. An understanding of the preschool child's needs, cognitive abilities, psychosocial crises, and moral and social development can greatly enhance book selection(22). Where the child fits within a developmental scheme gives a clue to the child's concerns and needs at that time. Most three-year-olds would be willing to listen to a book about a character being toilet trained; however, the use of such a book would fill a developmental need for some three-year-olds, but not for others who conquered toilet training at the age of two. Therefore, the helper selecting materials for use with a preschool child must be aware of the child's specific developmental needs, not just developmental norms based on chronological age.

The adult selecting literature for use with the preschool child should, if possible, pick materials that the adult likes personally. If the guide has personal involvement with the story, an emotional reaction can more likely be drawn from listeners; this is particularly important as the helper working with a preschool child will be engaged in reading the book aloud. It is also best if the helper can select several similar books on a developmental theme, so the child has a voice in choosing the book with the greatest appeal. By using this strategy, a book is not forced upon a child with the implication, "It's good for you"(23).

The person responsible for book selection should be aware of other tools for evaluating literature as well. The preschool child, of course, needs a quite different book format than the older child. Six aspects felt to be important guides to book selection for early-childhood literature are:
1) Appealing illustrations, whether pictures or photographs, that enhance the text and make good use of color.
2) Interesting story content, which presupposes a logical development of events and portrays believable characters.
3) Useful information, that is within the range of the child's understanding.
4) Broad humor, which needs to be fairly obvious for the preschool child.
5) Surprise elements, to create suspense and sustain interest.
6) Appealing, recurring refrains, which contribute familiarity and delight the child(24).

Although an early-childhood book exhibiting all the previous criteria would probably be a rare find, the adult selecting books for a preschool child would do well to keep the six guidelines in mind. Years of research on children's literature have shown that the preferences of specific age groups have remained very stable through the years(25).

Using Literature to Meet
Developmental Needs

Once a book has been selected for a preschool child which deals with a developmental need of the child and seems to constitute good literature, the adult must consider how to make best use of the book. In order to aid the child in identifying with a story situation and with the characters in the story, the adult must try to encourage active participation in literature on the part of the child. This active participation involves listening enjoyment by the child and activities making use of motor skills, cognitive tasks, and verbal skills which follow the reading of the book.

Reading aloud to children. The preschool child is often engaged in learning pre-reading skills. Although a few precocious preschoolers may have the ability to read books themselves, the vast majority of children this age need to be read to. Therefore, the adult selecting books for a particular preschool child can increase the child's listening enjoyment by having knowledge of some fundamentals of reading aloud.

Even experienced readers often use some pre-presentation techniques to make a reading more effective. It is essential to read, or at least skim, the selection ahead of time(26). Attention must be given to the author's style, whether it be serious, humorous, etc. Personality traits of the book's characters, unusual words or phrases within the text, and high points of the plot should all be examined.

Adults who are inexperienced at reading aloud may want to practice a story several times before reading it aloud to a child. How to distinguish characters from one another during book dialogue is one consideration. Emphasis of important words and key punctuation marks is also important. The adult's level of pitch, tone of voice, and pace of reading all contribute to creating the mood of a piece of literature.

Observing responses. Reading aloud may generate many kinds of responses. Some of the child's responses may be spontaneous and are likely to reflect emotional involvement with the selection as it is being read. A child may make value judgements concerning the story; a story character's behavior might be criticized or applauded by the child who has become actively involved with the story plot. Joy, anger, envy, or relief may be expressed by a child after hearing a book which aids in identification with a character. Any and all responses to a book should be accepted and encouraged, extended by discussion when the occasion is right.

Utilizing follow-up activities. In using literature to meet the developmental needs of the preschool child, at times the adult guide merely needs to read a book aloud and observe the child's responses. Some children will respond easily to selections that interest them, showing response in their comments as well as in their facial expressions as they hear a story. Other children may need more encouragement in responding to the literature. The adult guide may decide to make use of follow-up activities in this case.

Utilizing certain activities after the reading of a book can definitely be an aid in getting a young child involved in a book. Follow-up activities may encourage the child to make use of motor skills, cognitive abilities, or verbal skills. Since there is continuous change in skill levels during the span of the early-childhood years, activities have to be matched to the developmental capabilities of a particular child. While many two- and three-year-olds may only be capable of drawing a picture of their families by making a series of scribbles, the child over four years of age usually can draw representations of houses, people, animals, and other objects(27).

Likewise role playing is better understood and more enjoyed by the older preschool child. Activities involving verbal skills must vary greatly for the two-year-old versus the child who is turning six.

A particular child's likes and dislikes must also be considered by the adult guide. Some preschool children love dramatic play while others may prefer artistic activities. An ideal situation would be for the adult to have more than one activity related to the reading of a book for the preschool child to choose from. Three types of activities are listed below; these follow-up responses to the reading of a book are various types of art activities, drama activities, and written responses. Some of these activities can be used after reading aloud a book to an individual preschool child, while other activities are better suited to a small group of preschool children. The follow-up activities are grouped according to the type of response that is called for from the child.

Art activities allow the preschool child's fine-motor coordination to work with perceptual, cognitive, and emotional development. While **painting and drawing** give children a foundation for symbolic representation, they also provide them with a valuable expressive outlet(28). For young children whose writing and reading skills are still underdeveloped, drawing and painting are ways of expressing their own very personal reactions to an experience. While the outgoing child may readily express verbal reactions to a story, the reactions of the shy child may be locked inside. With crayons or paints and paper, this child's feelings can be expressed nonverbally. It is generally felt that children should not try to produce perfect representations, but be free to express moods and feelings in their artistic endeavors(29).

Mobiles and collages may be constructed by the older preschool child with pictures or photographs. Key events or activities from a story, as well as pictures depicting characters, can be represented by a mobile or collage. Mood collages can also be an effective way for children to better understand the emotions expressed by characters in a story.

The creation of **puppets** can greatly enhance the imagination of a preschooler. Simple yet creative puppets may be constructed by using paper bags, socks, small boxes, or fruits and vegetables. When children design the facial features of the puppets, they should keep in mind the most important personality traits of the characters they wish to represent.

Dramatic activities are especially good for young children as dramatic play can contribute to cognitive, physical, social, and emotional development. An excellent way to begin creative dramatics is through **pantomine**, which is expression, action, and gesture without words. It stimulates use of the whole body and relieves participants of the added skill of having to think of dialogue(30). Pantomine can be developed around activities, mood and feeling, and characterization. Pantomining an activity from a book is probably the best starting point for the preschooler. Pantomine focused specifically on mood and feeling can lead toward characterization and an attempt to combine expression, gesture, and movement to create a believable character or personality.

Role play, in particular, makes use of drama to solve particular social or emotional problems. It is somewhat related to therapy but differs vastly in degree and intensity(31). It sets up a problem situation for children to come to grips with and allows them to "play through" the problem in order to discover alternate solutions and the results of those solutions. Role playing may be considered preventive in that it provides an opportunity for all children in a group to develop sensitivity toward the feelings of others, and encourages changes of attitude through understanding(32).

Puppetry provides an outlet for different kinds of creativity; children not only develop and participate in the drama but construct the puppet as well. Puppetry is less threatening than other forms of dramatic activity for children who are shy. The puppet, an extension of the self, serves as a mask, enabling the player to gain a freedom which cannot be achieved when acting a part. The timid child can lose inhibitions and enter into the drama without self-consciousness(33).

Written responses to literature, although generally associated with the older child, can also be adapted for use with the preschool child. Certain preschool children can **dictate materials** which are written down by the helper. Dictation activities must be kept simple and involve a short time span for the child this age. Composing a short letter to a book character or a different ending for a story places the child on a personal level with the book. By dictating different types of materials to the helper, the child's cognitive and language involvement are enlisted. The child can not only perhaps identify with a story character, but may be able to come up with alternate solutions for dealing with problems. Children may like their own variations on a story theme so much, they will ask to hear them read again and again.

Word charts are another perhaps easier activity for the helper and the preschool child to participate in. The helper can write down lists of the child's likes and dislikes concerning story characters and incidents or have the child supply various words to describe pictures cut from magazines. Simple diagrams such as family trees or a child's daily schedule can be filled in with words written by the helper and accompanying pictures provided by the preschool child.

Follow-up activities involving the use of art, drama, or written responses can be an effective means of helping a preschool child identify with a story character or situation. Although discussed very generally in this chapter, more specific follow-up activities are listed in each of the later chapters of this book. Again it is stressed that the skill levels and age of a particular child be considered when using activities following the reading of a book. At times, a well-planned discussion may be all that is needed to enlist the preschool child's active participation in a story. Follow-up activities making use of art, drama, or written responses, however, can be a useful device for involving other children. Hopefully this active participation will lead to the child's identification with the story situation and help the child cope with developmental needs.

Conclusion

Since bibliotherapy is a useful tool for helping children meet developmental needs, among other uses, it seems most appropriate for literature to be read to the preschool child for this purpose. The early-childhood or preschool years, generally referred to as the years from two to six, encompass a period of vast developmental change. The chapters which follow reflect these areas of change in physical, motor, social, and emotional development encountered by the preschool child. A subsequent chapter, MOTOR DEVELOPMENT AND PHYSICAL CHANGE, discusses the preschool child's awareness of differences in size and motor capabilities; books which reflect this awareness are a part of the chapter. A chapter on SPECIAL DEVELOPMENTAL NEEDS includes material on the handicapped child and the child needing such devices as glasses or a hearing aid; selected books on these special needs are included.

The two- to six-year-old child is faced with the task of coping with emotions ranging from intense anger to pure joy. Due to the great strides in emotional development which occur during these early years, books about ANGER AND OTHER EMOTIONS and a discussion of these feelings comprise one chapter. The preschooler usually has one or more fears to conquer and possesses a love for fantasy; therefore, one chapter is made up of material and selected books on FEAR AND FANTASY.

The behavior patterns, attitudes, and values first encountered at this stage of life may be maintained for years(34). A chapter on ATTITUDES AND VALUES discusses these issues and includes children's books dealing with this developmental need. SELF-IMAGE AND SEX ROLES are covered in one chapter along with books dealing with these two important issues in a preschool child's development.

Three other chapters cover the very important relationships which a preschool child begins to develop. One is on FAMILY RELATIONSHIPS with material concerning the child's place within the family and books about this same topic. Other children's books deal with the more specific area of SINGLE-PARENT AND BLENDED FAMILIES, with pertinent information presented on the needs of many preschool children faced with these types of family situations. The two- to six-year-old also ventures outside the family to form relationships involving PEERS AND SCHOOL; a discussion and selected children's literature are therefore included on this third aspect of social development.

The developmental themes which are evident in early-childhood literature can be a valuable aid in helping children of this age group. A knowledge of the major theories of development can help the adult guide in selecting appropriate literature; however, the individual developmental pace of the child must always be considered. No longer is children's literature treated as though it did not exist in the same world as that in which our children's lives are lived(35). The very real developmental needs of preschool children can certainly be explored and understood through the use of bibliotherapy.

NOTES

1. Patricia Cionciolo, "Children's Literature Can Affect Coping Behavior," **Personnel and Guidance Journal** (Volume 43, 1965): 897–903.

2. Jean A. Pardeck and John T. Pardeck, "Bibliotherapy Using a Neo-Freudian Approach for Children of Divorced Parents," **The School Counselor** (Volume 32, No. 4, 1985): 313–318; John T. Pardeck and Jean A. Pardeck, "Bibliotherapy: An Approach to Helping Young People with Problems," **Journal of Group Psychotherapy, Psychodrama, and Sociometry** (Volume 37, No. 1, 1984): 41–43; John T. Pardeck and Jean A. Pardeck, "Treating Abused Children Through Bibliotherapy," **Early Child Development and Care** (Volume 16, Nos. 3 and 4, 1984): 195–204.

3. Carter Good, **Dictionary of Education** (Springfield, Massachusetts: Merriam, 1966), p. 212.

4. Barbara Lindeman and Martin Kling, "Bibliotherapy: Definitions, Uses, and Studies," **Journal of School Psychology** (Volume 2, 1969): 36–41.

5. Frederick A. Schrank and Dennis W. Engels, "Bibliotherapy as a Counseling Adjunct: Research Findings," **The Personnel and Guidance Journal** (Volume 60, 1981): 143–147.

6. George D. Spache, **Good Reading for Poor Readers** 9th ed. (Champaign, Illinois: Garrard Publishing, 1974), p. 21.

7. Joanne E. Bernstein, **Books to Help Children Cope with Separation and Loss** 2d ed. (New York: R.R. Bowker, 1983), p. 22.

8. Caroline Shrodes, **Bibliotherapy: A Theoretical and Clinical-Experimental Study** (Doctoral Dissertation: University of California, 1949).

9. Jean A. Pardeck and John T. Pardeck, **Young People with Problems: A Guide to Bibliotherapy** (Westport, Connecticut: Greenwood Press, 1984), p. 3.

10. Margaret Hannigan and William Henderson, "Narcotics Addicts Take Up Reading," **The Bookmark** (Volume 22, 1963): 281–284.

11. Pardeck and Pardeck, **Young People with Problems**, pp. 4–6.

12. Linda W. Craighead, Kathleen McNamara, and John J. Horan, "Perspectives on Self-Help and Bibliotherapy: You Are What You Read," in **Handbook of Counseling Psychology**, edited by Steven D. Brown and Robert W. Lent (New York: John Wiley and Sons, 1984), p. 918.

13. Frank Fischer, "Influence of Reading and Discussion on Attitudes of Fifth Graders Towards American Indians," **Journal of Educational Research** (Volume 62, 1968): 25–32.

14. Pardeck and Pardeck, **Young People with Problems**, p. 3.

15. David H. Russell and Caroline Shrodes, "Contributions of Research in Bibliotherapy to the Language-Arts Program," **School Review** (Volume 58, 1950): 411–420.

16. Barbara M. Neuman and Phillip R. Neuman, **Development Through Life: A Psychosocial Approach** 3d ed. (Homewood, Illinois: The Dorsey Press, 1984), p. 24.

17. Neuman and Neuman, pp. 7–10.

18. John W. Santrock and Steven R. Yussen, **Children and Adolescents-A Developmental Perspective** (Dubuque, Iowa: William C. Brown, 1984), pp. 44–45.

19. Santrock and Yussen, pp. 44–45.

20. Zena Sutherland, Dianne Monson, and May Hill Arbuthnot, **Children and Books** 6th ed. (Glenview, Illinois: Scott, Foresman, and Company, 1981), p. 29.

21. Sutherland, Monson, and Arbuthnot, p. 17.

22. Sutherland, Monson, and Arbuthnot, p. 19.

23. Bernstein, p. 35.

24. Margaret C. Gillespie and John W. Conner, **Creative Growth through Literature for Children and Adolescents** (Columbus, Ohio: Charles E. Merrill, 1975), p. 58.

25. Gillespie and Conner, pp. 57–58.

26. Sutherland, Monson, and Arbuthnot, p. 518.

27. Grace J. Craig, **Human Development** 2d ed. (Englewood Cliffs, New Jersey: Prentice Hall, 1980), p. 245.

28. Craig, p. 244.

29. Craig, p. 249.

30. Myra Sadker and David Sadker, **Now Upon a Time: A Contemporary View of Children's Literature** (New York: Harper and Row, 1977), p. 393.

31. Sadker and Sadker, p. 395.

32. Nellie McCaslin, **Creative Dramatics in the Classroom** (New York: McKay, 1968), p. 8.

33. McCaslin, p. 59.

34. Craig, p. 252.

35. Sutherland, Monson, and Arbuthnot, p. 16.

2

Anger and Other Emotions

Emotions of preschool children differ markedly from those of children in other stages of development. It is important that adults be aware of these differences. It also should be recognized by adults that children at the same stage of development do not necessarily have similar emotional patterns. Differences are inevitable due to learning opportunities and other unique experiences of the child. Even though individual differences in the emotional development of preschool children are evident, these differences are minimal if compared with the emotional development of older children.

A number of clear emotional patternings begin to emerge during the preschool time period. In particular, fear is an emotion that the child begins to deal with more effectively and anger is expressed more often(1). Jealousy is a normal response of children during this time period. Children must learn to deal with the emotions of shyness, sadness, and other feelings as well. Professionals who work with preschool children realize that anger, jealousy and other emotions are important ingredients to a child's overall development. These emotions are normal and children should be taught to deal with them effectively.

Anger

The frequency and intensity of anger in preschool children vary from child to child. Some children can deal more effectively with anger-provoking stimuli than others. The ability to deal with these stimuli varies according to the need that is being blocked, the child's emotional and physical condition at the time, and the situation in which the stimuli occur(2). Certain children may react to petty annoyance with anger; others may react with withdrawal; and still other children may not react to anger-provoking stimuli at all. Each child is unique and deals with environmental stimuli in certain ways.

Preschool children are angered by many of the same conditions that anger the infant. They especially resent interference with their possessions(3) and they fight continually with other children who grab their toys or interfere with their play activities. Preschool children become angry when toys or other objects do not work as they want them to and when they make mistakes in what they are attempting to do. In addition, preschool children become angry when they are ordered to do something they do not want to do at that moment.

Anger responses. Children have two major responses to anger: impulsive and inhibited. Impulsive responses are usually aggressive. They are directed against persons, objects, or even animals. They may be verbal or physical. Violent outbursts of anger or temper tantrums are most indicative of young children. It is not unusual for the preschool child to express anger through hitting, biting, kicking, punching, poking, and pulling. About the age of four years, language is added to the physical responses to anger in young children.

Impulsive expressions of anger are obviously more common than inhibited expressions. However some children do respond to anger in an inhibited way and consequently keep their anger under control or "bottled up." Inhibited responses are reflected in children who withdraw into themselves, feel sorry for themselves, or appear to be generally apathetic. Some children respond to anger in an inhibited fashion because they learn that this is the most effective way of dealing with anger. Impulsive and inhibited responses to anger are the normal ways that children deal with anger. Both responses to anger play an important role in the development of children.

Children learn to control the ways they respond to anger through interaction with other children. Naturally adults play a role in this learning process as well; however, it is difficult to learn appropriate responses to anger from someone who is bigger and more capable of dealing effectively with anger(4). Children who respond to anger in an impulsive way may very well lack exposure to the kinds of interactions with peers that teach a youngster how to properly express and control impulsive responses to anger. Consequently, other children, in particular the peer group, are effective teachers for showing appropriate responses to anger.

Nursery school or the preschool environment plays an important role in teaching the child ways to respond to anger. David J. Hicks found that when small children were exposed to an aggressive experience such as viewing an inflated doll being struck with a bat, mallet, or other object, those children imitated this behavior in their play after the exposure to aggression(5).

A study by Gerald R. Patterson also found results similar to those of Hicks. Patterson studied over 2,500 children in nursery school settings and concluded that aggressive responses to anger were strongly reinforced and taught by other children in the nursery school setting(6). One should keep in mind that experiences with peers play a major role in teaching children appropriate ways to respond to anger; yet it should be realized that each child is different and that the child's past history and personality are also factors that play an important part in this process.

Other Emotions

Jealousy, shyness, and sadness are emotions likely to impact development during the early-childhood years. Like anger, these emotions are typical of many children and must be dealt with by the child. There are some common patternings in the ways that children deal with jealousy, shyness, and sadness; however, each child is unique and may deal with these emotions much differently than other children.

Jealousy. Jealousy is a normal response to supposed, actual, or threatened loss of affection. It is an outgrowth of anger, giving rise to an attitude of resentment directed toward people. Fear may also combine with anger in the jealousy pattern. The jealous child feels insecure and is afraid of losing affection from others. Jealousy is created through situations social in nature; three main sources have been identified.

First, most jealousy during the early-childhood stage of development is homegrown, that is, it exists in the conditions originating in the family environment. For example, a new baby may take much of the time and attention away from the older child who has become accustomed to receiving it; the older sibling may thus feel neglected. The older child will feel resentful toward not only the new baby, but also the parents.

Second, if the preschool child comes from a home environment that engenders jealousy, this may carry over to the school environment. Not only are other children viewed as a threat by the child, but also the teacher. When the child develops relationships with other children in the school environment, anger may occur if someone else shows an interest in that child's friends. Jealousy may also flare up when the teacher compares the child with classmates or with an older sibling.

A third situation contributing to the development of jealousy is when the child feels deprived of material possessions. This would be a fairly advanced response and would be most typical of the five- or six-year-old child. This response can be particularly pronounced between siblings. Siblings must learn to deal with jealousy resulting from envy about toys and other material possessions important to the preschool years. Parents are important teachers in this learning process(7).

Shyness. Shyness is a form of fear characterized by shrinking from contact with others who are strange and unfamiliar. Few children escape an occasional experience of shyness. Preschool children may be shy in the presence of a guest in the home, a new baby-sitter, or a new teacher. They may experience shyness when their parents or peers are in the audience and they recite or participate in other ways in front of a group. Their shyness comes from uncertainty about how others may react to them, or fear that others will laugh at them.

Children show their shyness by stuttering, by talking as little as possible, or by nervous mannerisms such as pulling at their clothing or shifting from one foot to the other, and bending the head to one side and then raising it coyly to look at a strange person they have not seen before.

As children grow older, shyness becomes less intense and of briefer duration. If, however, shyness is extremely intense and frequent, it may lead to a generalized timidity that affects the child's social development and relationships with others. However, shyness is a predictable part of the developmental process experienced in varying degrees by all children(8).

Sadness. For most children sadness is experienced less than most other emotions. There are at least two reasons for this: 1) parents and teachers try to insulate children as much as possible from situations that contribute to sadness, and 2) very young children have short memories and their attention can easily be diverted to something more pleasant.

As the child grows older, the child is more apt to be confronted with situations that trigger sadness. Also, their memories improve, and diverting their attention to other more pleasant situations becomes more difficult. In essence, sadness is an emotional response that is less likely to occur than other emotions. Occasionally the preschool child is apt to experience sadness; however, for the most part, the child's attention can easily be redirected toward more pleasant feelings by the understanding adult(9).

Anger, jealousy, shyness, and sadness are all emotions that occur in children during the early-childhood period. Of these, sadness is the least likely to occur; however, it is an emotion that is important to the developmental process. All of the emotions discussed above are apt to occur in some form in children; the important issue is that the preschool child should learn how to deal with them effectively.

Anger and Other Emotions in Early
Childhood Literature

Between the ages of two and six, children develop dominant coping strategies--methods of dealing with their feelings--that may last a lifetime(10). The emotions of anger, jealousy, shyness, and sadness are all encountered by preschool children; these same emotions are portrayed in children's literature. In particular, anger and a character's responses to it are a common theme in picture books. One source of anger is within the child's own family; a book character may be angry about parental requests or about being denied something that is wanted. A very young character may resort to a temper tantrum, while an older preschool child may become sullen or threaten to run away. Anger directed toward peers is found in many books for preschool children as well. In picture books, the hostility that can prevent or mar a friendship is very realistically portrayed(11). Responding to anger felt toward peers or siblings may involve physical aggression such as hitting, biting, and kicking.

Jealousy is another emotion which is prevalent in early-childhood books. Characters may be envious of their friend's toys and other possessions. Books dealing with the arrival of a new sibling within a household invariably depict the older child as feeling jealousy toward the new baby. Feelings of shyness are experienced by certain characters who encounter new people within their home or a new situation such as starting school. Disappointment and sadness are also dealt with when characters experience friends moving away or parents giving them less time and attention than usual.

Responses to the literature. With the many children's books available illustrating various common emotions, a child can be helped in developing ways to cope with emotions. Most books stress that feelings should be expressed rather than denied. Although aggressive acts such as hitting and kicking are very realistically portrayed in some of these books, other more positive ways of dealing with emotions are illustrated as well.

Many of the books concerning various emotions show a character seeking out an adult who is generally able to make the child feel somewhat better. An adult guide reading such a book to a child can assist the child in exploring various feelings through responses to the literature such as:
1. Having the child choose a color which describes the child's feelings at that time.
2. Constructing paper plate faces or masks with yarn, colored paper, and so on to express various feelings and moods.
3. Pantomining of a particular feeling by a child, with other children or an adult trying to identify it.
4. Having the child supply short answers to statements such as: I feel _____ when someone scolds me; I feel _____ when I get up in the morning; I feel _____ when someone else wins a game; I feel _____ when a toy gets broken.
5. Finding magazine pictures of people, identifying what emotion they may be feeling, and speculating as to why they feel that way(12).

Since the preschool years are such an important time for children to develop coping strategies for their emotions, the use of literature dealing with these emotions seems quite useful. The child's emotions related to the family and peer group need to be explored and better understood so that the child can respond to these feelings in a productive fashion. Early-childhood literature which deals with such emotions as anger, jealousy, shyness, or sadness would certainly appear to facilitate positive emotional growth in the preschool child.

NOTES

1. Elizabeth B. Hurlock, **Child Development** 6th ed. (New York: McGraw-Hill, 1978), p. 202.
2. Hurlock, p. 202.
3. Hurlock, p. 203.
4. Julius Segal and Herbert Yahraes, **A Child's Journey** (New York: McGraw-Hill, 1979), p. 240.
5. David J. Hicks, "Imitation and Retention of Film-Mediated Aggressive Peer and Adult Models," **Journal of Personality and Social Psychology** (Volume 2, 1965): 97-100.
6. G. Patterson, R. Littman, and W. Bricker, "Assertive Behavior in Children: A Step Toward a Theory of Aggression," **Monographs of the Society for Research in Child Development** (Volume 32, No. 5, 1967): 1-43.

7. Hurlock, pp. 203-204.

8. Hurlock, pp. 199-200.

9. Hurlock, p. 205.

10. Grace J. Craig, **Human Development** 2d ed. (Englewood Cliffs, New Jersey: Prentice-Hall, 1980), p. 252.

11. Myra Sadker and David Sadker, **Now Upon a Time-A Contemporary View of Children's Literature** (New York: Harper and Row, 1977), p. 297.

12. Laura Broad and Nancy Butterworth, **The Playgroup Handbook** (New York: St. Martin's Press, 1974); Don Dinkmeyer, **Developing Understanding of Self and Others (DUSO) Manual** (Circle Pines, Minnesota: American Guidance Service, 1970); **Kindergarten Guide** (Cleveland: Diocesan Education Office, 1977).

BOOKS

2.1 Alden. **Saying I'm Sorry.** see Ch. 3.

2.2 Alexander. **When the New Baby Comes, I'm Moving Out.** see Ch. 4.

2.3 Andersen. **What's the Matter, Sylvie, Can't You Ride?** see Ch. 8.

2.4 Anderson, Penny. **Feeling Frustrated.** Chicago: Children's Press, 1982. 29 pp.

Various situations which can leave a child feeling frustrated are described--accidents, disappointment over a broken promise, the inability to perform certain tasks, being unable to find a possession, hearing too many "don'ts" from parents. It is stressed that having someone such as an adult understand one's frustration can help a child feel better.

IL: Ages 4-6

2.5 Armitage, Ronda and David. **The Bossing of Josie.** London: Andre Deutsch, 1980. 28 pp.

Feeling she is constantly bossed by her parents and older sister, Josie attempts to boss her baby brother but he ignores her. On her birthday, Josie receives a witch's costume and decides to get back at her family by casting spells on all of them. Momentarily pleased and later upset when she believes she has caused her brother to disappear, Josie is relieved when he comes out of hiding. Josie decides to only cast good spells in the future.

IL: Ages 4-6

2.6 Banish. **I Want to Tell You About My Baby.** see Ch. 4.

2.7 Barsuhn, Rochelle. **Feeling Angry.** Chicago: Children's Press, 1982. 29 pp.

Disagreeing with friends, having a toy broken by someone else, needing to clean up, being ignored--these are all times when a child may feel anger toward someone or something. Positive ways of overcoming anger and making it a short-term feeling are discussed.

IL: Ages 4-6

2.8 Berenstain. **The Berenstain Bears Get in a Fight.** see Ch. 4.

2.9 Bottner, Barbara. **Mean Maxine.** New York: Random House, 1980. 29 pp.

Ralph is upset by Maxine's name-calling, so his brother advises him to stand up to Maxine. As he practices telling off Maxine, Ralph fantasizes breathing fire on her, swallowing her like a whale, and locking her in a dungeon. When Ralph actually meets up with Maxine and tries to scare her, she asks him for pointers on being a monster and the two decide to play together.

IL: Ages 4-6

2.10 Brandenberg, Aliki. **Feelings.** New York: Greenwillow Books, 1984. 32 pp.

Pictures and short stories illustrate a full range of emotions in children--fear, anger, jealousy, and sadness as well as joy and love. Peer and sibling relationships are explored. It is stressed that feelings can't always be seen or heard.

IL: Ages 4-6

2.11 Brandenberg. **We Are Best Friends.** see Ch. 7.

2.12 Carlson. **Harriet and Walt.** see Ch. 4.

2.13 Chess. **Poor Esme.** see Ch. 5.

2.14 Chorao, Kay. **Kate's Box.** New York: E.P. Dutton, 1982. 21 pp.

When Kate discovers that her baby cousin is coming to visit, she hides in a box. Just as she remembered from last time, the baby captures everyone's attention. However, when her baby cousin starts to cry and others leave the room, only Kate is able to make the baby happy.

IL: Ages 2-4

2.15 Chorao, Kay. **Kate's Quilt.** New York: E.P. Dutton, 1982. 21 pp.

When Kate's surprise present from her mother turns out to be a quilt instead of a dolly, Kate is disappointed and throws a tantrum. Mother wisely ignores Kate's behavior. That evening, however, when Kate feels cold and is frightened, she appreciates the warmth and security her new quilt provides.

IL: Ages 2-4

2.16 Cole. **The New Baby at Your House.** see Ch. 4.

2.17 Cooney. **The Blanket that Had to Go.** see Ch. 8.

2.18 Corey, Dorothy. **New Shoes.** Chicago: Albert Whitman and Company, 1985. 28 pp.

When everyone else in the family gets new shoes, a little girl impatiently waits to outgrow her own. She jealously examines all her friends' new shoes and even attempts to lose her shoes. Finally her shoes grow too tight and the little girl and her mother go on an exciting shoe hunting expedition.

IL: Ages 4-6

2.19 Crary. **I Can't Wait.** see Ch. 3.

2.20 Crary. **My Name is not Dummy.** see Ch. 7.

2.21 Davis. **The Other Emily.** see Ch. 8.

2.22 Delton. **I Never Win.** see Ch. 8.

2.23 Delton. **Lee Henry's Best Friend.** see Ch. 7.

2.24 Delton. **My Mother Lost Her Job Today.** see Ch. 9.

2.25 Dillon. **The Beast in the Bed.** see Ch. 5.

2.26 Dragonwagon. **Always, Always.** see Ch. 9.

2.27 Dragonwagon. **I Hate My Brother Harry.** see Ch. 4.

2.28 Eriksson, Eva. **Jealousy.** Minneapolis: Carolrhoda Books, 1985. 24 pp.

Victor and Rosalie are very best friends and constant companions until Rosalie becomes ill with the mumps. Once Rosalie is well, she eagerly searches for Victor only to find him busily playing with a new friend Sophie. Quite jealous of Sophie, Rosalie tries to exclude her from games and fantasizes about her demise. When Victor gets lost during hide and seek, however, the two girls start laughing and having so much fun they decide to try a threesome once Victor returns.

IL: Ages 4-6

2.29 Frankel. **The Family of Tiny White Elephants.** see Ch. 4.

2.30 Fujikawa, Gyo. **Sam's All-Wrong Day.** New York: Grosset and Dunlap, 1982. 24 pp.

Sam's day seems to go wrong right from the start--he steps on the dog's tail, breaks an egg, stubs his toe, gets bitten by mosquitoes, and ruins his lunch. However, he does enjoy picking strawberries with his friends who encourage Sam that things can only get better. When the friends later discover a bear cub eating their pails of strawberries, Sam is the only one with a plan to scare it away and the rest of the day seems just fine.

IL: Ages 4-6

2.31 Galbraith. **Katie Did!** see Ch. 4.

2.32 Hamilton. **Big Sisters are Bad Witches.** see Ch. 4.

2.33 Hamilton, Morse. **How Do You Do, Mr. Birdsteps?** New York: Avon Books, 1983. 27 pp.

Too shy to meet her parents' dinner guest, four year old Kate goes to her bedroom and talks things over with her doll Zoe. When the guest plays the piano, Kate reluctantly ventures out of her room to hear the music. Claiming her doll is shy, Kate has Zoe converse with the man and he plays another song just for them.

IL: Ages 4-6

2.34 Hargreaves, Roger. **Mr. Grumpy.** Mankato, Minnesota: Creative Education, 1980. 31 pp.

Mr. Grumpy is so ill-tempered he tears pages out of books and pulls up all the pretty flowers in his garden. Scheming to improve Mr. Grumpy's outlook, Mr. Happy enlists the aid of his friend Mr. Tickle. After a day of being followed and tickled by the long arms of Mr. Tickle, Mr. Grumpy decides to try being nicer to everyone, including himself.

IL: Ages 4-6

2.35 Harris. **I Hate Kisses.** see Ch. 3.

2.36 Hawkins. **Snap! Snap!** see Ch. 5.

2.37 Hayes. **Patrick and Ted.** see Ch. 7.

2.38 Hazen, Barbara. **It's a Shame about the Rain: The Bright Side of Disappointment.** New York: Human Sciences Press, 1982. 29 pp.

A young boy feels disappointed when a heavy rain cancels his family's plans for a picnic at the lake. After a display of anger, the boy sadly curls up on his bed and talks to his mother about how everyone feels disappointment at times, even grownups. Meanwhile the boy's father brightens the gloomy day by organizing a fireside picnic followed by a building project the whole family participates in.

IL: Ages 4-6

2.39 Hazen, Barbara. **Very Shy.** New York: Human Sciences Press, 1982. 30 pp.

Nancy, who is painfully shy at school and around new people, wonders why she feels so at ease with her parents, her best friends, or when playing make-believe. Both of Nancy's parents claim they were shy as children and they gently try to encourage Nancy to speak up at school. When a new boy at school proves to be just as shy as Nancy, the two begin talking each day and eventually encourage each other to approach new playmates.

IL: Ages 4-6

2.40 Henkes, Kevin. **All Alone.** New York: Greenwillow Books, 1981. 26 pp.

A young child discusses the advantages of being alone: one can hear more and see more, pretend to be a different size, think about favorite events, etc. Being alone is also viewed as a good time for self-examination and to discover one's uniqueness from others. Although the child also enjoys being with friends, an appreciation for being alone is expressed too.

IL: Ages 4-6

2.41 Hines. **Maybe a Band-Aid Will Help.** see Ch. 4.

2.42 Hoffman. **Sister Sweet Ella.** see Ch. 4.

2.43 Horner. **Little Big Girl.** see Ch. 6.

2.44 Joosse. **The Thinking Place.** see Ch. 3.

2.45 Keller. **Too Big.** see Ch. 4.

2.46 Kempler, Rappaport, Spirn. **A Man Can Be...** see Ch. 8.

2.47 Kherdian, David and Nonny Hogrogian. **Right Now.** New York: Alfred A. Knopf, 1983. 25 pp.

A little girl describes feelings she has had in the past--sadness, anger, disappointment, and pain. She also daydreams about future events such as going to the zoo, a new teacher at school, purchasing a new coat. However, the little girl realizes that instead of dwelling too much on the past or future, she should make the most of what is happening "right now."

IL: Ages 4-6

2.48 Lakin. **Don't Touch My Room.** see Ch. 4.

2.49 Lalli, Judy. **Feelings Alphabet: An Album of Emotions from A to Z.** Rolling Hills Estates, CA: B.L. Winch, 1984. 57 pp.

Each letter of the alphabet is used to start a word depicting a feeling or emotion, accompanied by photographs of children.

IL: Ages 4-6

2.50 Lasky. **A Baby for Max.** see Ch. 4.

2.51 Lindgren. **I Want a Brother or Sister.** see Ch. 4.

2.52 Lindgren, Barbro. **Sam's Lamp.** New York: William Morrow and Company, 1983. 24 pp.

An adventurous Sam is able to climb to the top of the table to reach for a lamp. When Sam falls, he cries and is angry at the lamp until mother comforts him.

IL: Ages 2-4

2.53 Lindgren, Barbro. **Sam's Teddy Bear.** New York: William Morrow and Company, 1982. 26 pp.

Although Sam can be affectionate with his teddy bear, he also likes to bite it and throw it out of bed. Afraid that he has hurt his teddy, which falls in the potty, Sam cries until his dog rescues it and puts the teddy back in bed.

IL: Ages 2-4

2.54 Lindsay. **Do I Have a Daddy?** see Ch. 9.

2.55 Luttrell, Ida. **Lonesome Lester.** New York: Harper and Row, 1984. 38 pp.

Although he longs for some company, Lester the prairie dog discovers there are problems involved when some ants, his Aunt Martha, and a baby rabbit come to visit. Lester is polite to all his guests and works hard to make each feel welcome. Lester finds that when his last guest is gone, however, that he enjoys solitary activities and appreciates his chance to be alone once again.

IL: Ages 4-6

2.56 Noble. **Where Do I Fit In?** see Ch. 9.

2.57 O'Brien. **Come Play with Us.** see Ch. 7.

2.58 O'Brien. **I Want That!** see Ch. 3.

2.59 Oram, Hiawyn. **Angry Arthur.** New York: Harcourt Brace Jovanovich, 1982. 27 pp.

Angered by his mother's request that he go to bed, Arthur proceeds to destroy his home, the neighborhood, and eventually the planet Earth. Although his mother, father, and both grandparents admonish Arthur by saying "That's enough," Arthur is still so angry he wrecks the entire universe. Crawling into his bed which is floating in space, Arthur finds he can't remember what he grew so angry about.

IL: Ages 4-6

2.60 Oxenbury, Helen. **The Birthday Party.** New York: E.P. Dutton, 1983. 16 pp.

A child helps pick out a birthday present, then wants to try it out herself before the party. Once at the party, she is reluctant to hand over the present but starts having a good time with the other children. As the little girl is ready to leave the party, the birthday child doesn't want to share balloons with departing guests.

IL: Ages 2-4

2.61 Rogers. **Going to Day Care.** see Ch. 7.

2.62 Rogers. **The New Baby.** see Ch. 4.

2.63 Sharmat, Marjorie. **Atilla the Angry.** New York: Holiday House, 1985. 29 pp.

Known for his bad temper, Atilla Squirrel is avoided by his friends when he gets angry at objects, other animals, etc. Realizing he needs help, Atilla attends a club meeting for angry animals where he gets pointers on squashing his angry thoughts. Atilla follows the advice with some success, but he finally has to unleash his pent-up anger. Atilla and his friends decide that although anger can often be replaced with pleasant thoughts, at times everyone gets mad and that's OK too.

IL: Ages 4-6

2.64 Sharmat. **Come Home, Wilma.** see Ch. 5.

2.65 Sharmat, Marjorie. **Grumley the Grouch.** New York: Holiday House, 1980. 29 pp.

Grumley the badger has the reputation of being the biggest grouch in the neighborhood. When his house gets flooded, Grumley tries to stay at two different friends' homes but neither situation works out because of his grouchiness. When Grumley meets another badger, Brunhilda, who is just as grouchy as he is, the two become friends and are eventually able to discover some things they like.

IL: Ages 4-6

2.66 Sharmat. **Rollo and Juliet, Forever!** see Ch. 7.

2.67 Sharmat, Marjorie. **Twitchell the Wishful.** New York: Holiday House, 1981. 34 pp.

Twitchell the mouse envies all his friends' belongings and declares he can't be happy unless he has all the things he wants. He is momentarily overjoyed then when Twitchell's friends arrive at his doorstep to present him with their admired possessions. After a visit to another wiser friend, Twitchell discovers he really doesn't need or want his friends' possessions as much as he thought. He returns the items and goes home to enjoy his own things.

IL: Ages 4-6

2.68 Shyer. **Stepdog.** see Ch. 9.

2.69 Soderstrom. **Maybe Tomorrow I'll Have a Good Time.** see Ch. 7.

2.70 Stinson. **Mom and Dad Don't Live Together Any More.** see Ch. 9.

2.71 Sheehan, Cilla. **The Colors That I Am.** New York: Human Sciences Press, 1981. 24 pp.

Feelings such as happiness and excitement are discussed, as well as sadness, anger, jealousy, fear, nervousness, and loneliness. Colors are used to describe each feeling and events which could produce each feeling are mentioned. The importance of sharing one's feelings with others is also stressed.

IL: Ages 4-6

2.72 Tester, Sylvia. **Frustrated.** Chicago: Children's Press, 1980. 31 pp.

A child experiences a frustrating day when everything seems to go wrong, from problems with clothing to a fight with a friend. Deciding that it's too difficult to deal with the frustration alone, the child turns to a parent to share the day's problems.

IL: Ages 4-6

2.73 Tester, Sylvia. **Jealous.** Chicago: Children's Press, 1980. 31 pp.

After the arrival of a baby brother, a young child is jealous and feels ignored by his family. The child slams the door, gets red in the face, and kicks the floor in response to his emotions. The child is helped when older siblings tell of jealous feelings they've had in the past and family members pay extra attention to the child.

IL: Ages 4-6

2.74 Tester, Sylvia. **Sad.** Chicago: Children's Press, 1980. 31 pp.

Feeling sorrow over the death of a pet, a child recalls other times when sadness has been experienced: when a friend moved away, when someone got hurt, when two friends quarrelled. Realizing that it's OK to feel sad--everyone does sometimes--the child seeks parental comfort.

IL: Ages 4-6

2.75 van der Meer. **I'm fed up!** see Ch. 5.

2.76 Van Leeuwen. **Amanda Pig and Her Big Brother Oliver.** see Ch. 4.

2.77 Walter. **My Mama Needs Me.** see Ch. 4.

2.78 Weiss, Ellen. **The Angry Book.** New York: Random House, 1983. 31 pp.

When her breakfast burns and all her friends seem to be keeping secrets from her, Temper Tantrum Turtle kicks and screams to show her anger. Still declaring that her friends are mean, Temper Tantrum Turtle is taken home by Loving Lion. There the turtle is overjoyed to discover her friends having a surprise party for her, but she throws a tantrum once again when the party's over.

IL: Ages 4-6

2.79 Weiss. **Chuckie.** see Ch. 4.

2.80 Wells. **Timothy Goes to School.** see Ch. 7.

2.81 Winthrop. **Katharine's Doll.** see Ch. 7.

2.82 Winthrop. **Tough Eddie.** see Ch. 8.

3

Attitudes and Values

For the preschool child, the most important teacher of attitudes and values is the family system. The learning of attitudes and values is an important part of the socialization process. As children begin to internalize the attitudes and values important to functioning successfully in society, they begin to develop a conscience that will impact their entire lives. This internalization of attitudes and values occurs very early in life and is often spontaneous; however, much of this process occurs through the identification with parents. Many of the attitudes and values that children internalize will be those of their parents. Another important influence in this process is the mass media, in particular the television. Several experts have argued that the television is one of the key competitors with parents in teaching attitudes and values(1). Presently, there is much debate surrounding the brutality and violence portrayed on television that suggest such behavior is acceptable. Certain children may begin to develop a value base where violence is an acceptable way of life. However, positive role models, in particular parents, appear to have a greater impact on real life than television.

Attitudes of Small Children

Parental attitudes influence the way parents treat their children, and their treatment of the children, in turn, influences their children's attitudes toward them and others. The importance of the parents' attitudes on the child is that these attitudes have a tendency to persist in the child throughout development. If the child has internalized favorable attitudes from parents, all to the good; however, unfavorable attitudes will persist as well and may impact development negatively(2).

In order to understand attitudes of small children, one must look closely at several issues related to the attitudes of the child's parents. Attitudes are totally learned from the child's environment; several factors have been identified that help one to understand this process:

1) Some parents prior to the birth of a child will develop a concept of what the child should be like. This concept is often highly romanticized and based on what parents would like their child to be. Many children fall short of these parental expectations. Parents

become disappointed and this encourages the development of a rejectant attitude in the child.

2) Cultural values about the best way to treat children, whether in an authoritarian, democratic, or permissive way, will influence attitudes of parents toward the treatment of children. As children internalize these attitudes and grow to adulthood, they will probably have similar attitudes toward parenting. A parent's attitude toward parenting has a tremendous impact on the child's social and emotional development.

3) Parents who enjoy parenting will often reflect positive attitudes toward their children. Naturally, this in turn has a very favorable impact on the development of positive attitudes in the child.

4) How children react to parents influences the parents' attitudes toward them. If children show affection for and dependence on their parents, parents react to them very differently than they do when children are independent and more attached to outsiders than to the parents. This transactional process plays a key role in the child's social and emotional development(3).

Prejudice. Prejudice may be defined as "the negative attitudes directed toward members of social groups who are perceived by themselves and others in terms of racial, religious, national, or cultural-linguistic attributes"(4). Prejudice is unpleasant but has always been a part of humankind.

Prejudice has typically been defined as an adult attitude. However racial awareness begins to develop early, even during the preschool years. Prejudicial attitudes appear in children around the age of four. Obviously the greatest teachers of prejudice are parents and the peer group. As children grow older, their prejudices become more sophisticated, and often they have more stereotyped racial and ethnic attitudes than younger children(5).

Other attitudes. Given the fact that the preschool child's cognitive development is not very advanced, attitudes in general are not well developed. As pointed out in the discussion of prejudice, the most important teachers of attitudes are parents and the peer group in very young children. As the child matures, attitudes become clearer and more complex in the child.

Attitudes developed in the early-childhood years focus on responsibility, honesty, learning simple rules of etiquette, and so on. These attitudes are tremendously impacted by the home environment. Clearly if a child develops positive attitudes toward such attributes, total development will be enhanced.

Values of Small Children

The family system has the most influence on a child's value development(6). An important function of the family system is to transmit to the offspring the prescribed, permitted, and proscribed values of society and the acceptable means of achieving these values. Since values are transmitted socially, it is likely that children will have values similar to their parents or other significant individuals in the child's life.

Children during the preschool years do not have a highly developed value base governing their behavior. This is due to the fact that they are still learning the appropriate values of society and more importantly, that their cognitive development is still in the preoperational stage. This stage is a time period of egocentric thinking in which it is difficult for children to take the views of others and internalize values into the thinking process.

Learning appropriate socially approved values is a long, slow process that extends into adolescence. It is one of the most important developmental tasks of childhood. The preschool child is expected to have some sense of appropriate values prior to entering school. These values help the child distinguish between "right" and "wrong" and lay the foundation for the development of conscience. Before childhood is over, children are expected to develop a scale of values and a conscience to guide them when they must make a moral decision(7).

Piaget provides a great deal of insight into how values develop during the early-childhood years. According to Piaget, preschool children are in a period he called the "stage of moral realism" or "morality by constraint." During this stage, children's behavior is characterized by automatic obedience to rules without reasoning or judgement. Children during the preschool years largely regard parents and other adults in authority as omnipotent and follow the rules laid down without questioning their justice. In this moral stage of development, children judge acts as "right" or "wrong" in terms of consequences rather than motivation behind them. An act, for example, is regarded "wrong" because it results in punishment from other human beings or from natural or supernatural forces(8). Piaget's position clearly suggests that values play a limited role in governing behavior during the "stage of moral realism" or "morality by constraint."

Even though children's values during the preschool years are not well developed, they will obviously begin to cystallize as time passes. Parents and other significant adults in the child's life are the greatest teachers of these values. The internalization of socially approved values are critical in a child's overall development.

Prosocial behavior. Values and behavior are interrelated. Values lay the ground work governing a person's behavior. In the preschool child, the impact of values on behavior is not at its peak; however, as the child matures, values will play a greater role in shaping behavior.

The child in the preschool years is continually bombarded by values that promote prosocial behavior. The acceptance of these values is largely impacted by pressures from the social environment, specifically parents, peers, and teachers. As children are pressured toward prosocial values and behaviors, they will gradually correct unsocial patterns and thus become less selfish and demanding and more cooperative. Generosity and the ability to work and play cooperatively generally emerges by the time the child is around four years of age.

Unsocial behavior. Children quickly learn that to be accepted, they must conform to value and behavioral expectations of others. It is important to note that unsocial behaviors causing nonacceptance by others are an important part of the learning process. Through this process, children learn how others react to them and they learn that if they want to be accepted as members of the social group, they must conform to the group's values and behavioral expectations.

The process of changing unsocial values and behaviors depends on 1) how anxious the child is to be socially accepted, 2) the child's knowledge of how to change values and behaviors, and 3) growing intellectual ability which enables the child to see the relationship between values and behavior and social acceptance(9). It should be clearly evident that in the preschool child this process is not very sophisticated; however, at a very elementary level it is operating in the child. Obviously, the process of eliminating unsocial values and behaviors is an important part of development.

Attitudes and Values in Early Childhood Literature

Writers in the 1800s were convinced that through reading, a child would grow up to be good or bad and therefore provided morals at the end of stories. Although children's literature today does not preach sermons, many stories tell about a character who has a problem to solve. The older preschool child can ponder the decision the fictional character makes and identify with the same circumstances. Thus the child may begin to develop a sense of values(10).

First at home, then later in the neighborhood or in school, the young child learns with varying degrees of success how to live with others in interdependent relationships: helping as well as being helped, sharing, taking turns, following, leading. These children are learning to belong(11). Books which focus on these very elementary values essential for group living can aid the preschool child's social and emotional development. The preschool child begins to select playmates on the criteria of sex, racial and ethnic origins, and common interests; these are learned behaviors resulting from environmental conditioning(12). Picture story experiences with many ethnic groups and cultural mores may help to keep the young child's categories open-ended. Perhaps early explorations of attitudes and values through literature can set the pace for positive development in these areas in later years.

Responses to the literature. Although they are not as plentiful for this age group as for older children, there are an increasing number of early-childhood books available which focus on attitudes and values. Preschool children's needs to show responsibility for their own belongings within the home are stressed in some books. Learning to respect parental rules and those in group situations such as nursery school is another issue found in certain children's books. Sharing, taking turns, and being open-minded toward others are additional topics which can be found in literature for this age group. A helping individual can certainly explore this area of development with the preschooler by having the child:

1) Pantomine or use puppets to demonstrate inappropriate table manners, etc.

2) Pretend that there are no rules at home or at school and listing the consequences on a chart.

3) Draw or paint the aftereffects of certain behavior, such as pushing another child, talking back to an adult, or leaving a bike on the sidewalk or street.

4) Role play a nice way and a poor way to tell or ask someone--to not play with one's toys, to play a game fairly, to help clean up toys, and so on.

5) List things parents do for the child and checking off those the child feels could be done independently(13).

Although the development of attitudes and values is a continuous process for the child often thought to be centered in the middle school years and adolescence, the preschool child's development in this area is important as well. Around the age of four, children develop an awareness of parental attitudes and values concerning such issues as honesty, prejudice, and sharing. Although it is unrealistic to attempt to engage the preschool child in any type of detailed values clarification exercises, some preliminary exploration of attitudes and values would seem to enhance the preschooler's development.

NOTES

1. Advisory Committee on Child Development, **Toward a National Policy for Children and Families** (Washington, D.C.: National Academy of Sciences, 1976).

2. Elizabeth B. Hurlock, **Child Development** 6th ed. (New York: McGraw-Hill, 1978), p. 495.

3. Hurlock, p. 496.

4. H.M. Proshansky, "The Development of Intergroup Attitudes" in **Review of Child Development Research** Volume 2, edited by L.W. Hoffman and M.L. Hoffman (New York: Russell Sage Foundation, 1966), p. 311.

5. Grace J. Craig, **Human Development** 2d ed. (Englewood Cliffs, New Jersey: Prentice-Hall, 1980), p. 334.

6. Theodore Lidz, **The Person** (New York: Basic Books, 1976), p. 60.

7. R.J. Havighurst, **Human Development and Education** (New York: Longmans, 1953).

8. Hurlock, p. 390.

9. Hurlock, p. 238.

10. Nancy Larrick, **A Parent's Guide to Children's Reading** (New York: Bantam Books, 1975), p. 143-144.

11. Margaret C. Gillespie and John W. Conner, **Creative Growth through Literature for Children and Adolescents** (Columbus, Ohio: Charles E. Merrill, 1975), p. 68.

12. Gillespie and Conner, p. 68.

13. Don Dinkmeyer, **Developing Understanding of Self and Others** (DUSO) **Manual** (Circle Pines, Minnesota: American Guidance Service, 1970); Jean A. Pardeck and John T. Pardeck, **Young People with Problems: A Guide to Bibliotherapy** (Westport, Connecticut: Greenwood Press, 1984); Guy Wagner, Laura Gilloley, Betts Ann Roth, and Joan Cesinger, **Games and Activities for Early Childhood Education** (New York: Teachers Publishing, 1967).

BOOKS

3.1 Alda. **Sonya's Mommy Works.** see Ch. 8.

3.2 Alden, Laura. **Saying I'm Sorry.** Chicago: Children's Press, 1982. 29 pp.

Although it is recognized that saying "I'm sorry" can be quite difficult for a child, various situations where this phrase is appropriate are described. When one is late, after an accident, after hurting someone's feelings, after interrupting someone--all of these circumstances can be made better with an "I'm sorry." What to do when others are sorry is also discussed.

IL: Ages 4-6

3.3 Alexander. **We're in Big Trouble, Blackboard Bear.** see Ch. 7.

3.4 Barbato. **From Bed to Bus.** see Ch. 8.

3.5 Bauer. **My Mom Travels a Lot.** see Ch. 8.

3.6 Berenstain. **The Berenstain Bears and Mama's New Job.** see Ch. 8.

3.7 Berenstain, Stan and Jan. **The Berenstain Bears and the Messy Room.** New York: Random House, 1983. 29 pp.

Although the rest of the Bear family's house is neat and clean, Brother and Sister Bear's room is usually a cluttered, dusty mess. Tired of picking up after the children, Mama Bear loses her temper one day and proceeds to throw away their scattered possessions. Papa Bear restores peace in the family by making plans for how Brother and Sister Bear can better organize and classify their belongings.

IL: Ages 4-6

3.8 Berenstain, Stan and Jan. **The Berenstain Bears and the Truth.** New York: Random House, 1983. 29 pp.

Bored during a do-nothing day, Brother and Sister Bear challenge each other to play soccer inside, resulting in a broken lamp. The two siblings concoct a story to explain the broken lamp which they tell to Mama and repeat with variations to Papa Bear. Mama claims she is upset, not about the lamp, but about her two cubs perhaps not telling the truth. After spilling out the true story and each claiming to be at fault, Brother and Sister feel they have learned an important lesson.

IL: Ages 4-6

3.9 Berry, Joy. **Let's Talk About Being Rude.** Chicago: Children's Press, 1985. 31 pp.

Rude people are described as those who treat others as if they are not important, those who insist on being first, those who always want to have their way, and so on. Ways to keep from being rude are listed in turn, with consideration for others stressed as the key to avoiding rude behavior.

IL: Ages 4-6

3.10 Berry, Joy. **Let's Talk About Disobeying.** Chicago: Children's Press, 1982. 31 pp.

Disobeying is defined and reasons why parents or other adults make rules for children to follow are given--so a child won't get hurt or break a possession, as well as so he or she will have friends, learn fairness, etc. Children are encouraged to ask their parents questions if they are unsure about adult rules. Punishments such as isolation and withdrawal of privileges are discussed.

IL: Ages 4-6

3.11 Berry, Joy. **Let's Talk About Fighting.** Chicago: Children's Press, 1982. 29 pp.

Hurting each other's bodies or feelings, as well as damaging each other's possessions, are stated as the negative effects of fighting. Ways to avoid a fight, such as ignoring someone's teasing, are discussed. However, arguments cannot always be avoided; therefore, the merits of talking things out, compromising, and occasionally seeking adult help are stressed.

IL: Ages 4-6

3.12 Berry, Joy. **Let's Talk About Lying.** Chicago: Children's Press, 1985. 31 pp.

The act of lying is defined, as compared to making up stories for entertainment or telling an untruth by mistake. Reasons that children lie are discussed, as well as the results of lying--disappointing others, losing the trust of others. Ways to make things better, such as admitting the lie and apologizing for it, are also covered.

IL: Ages 4-6

3.13 Berry, Joy. **Let's Talk About Whining.** Chicago: Children's Press, 1984. 29 pp.

Reasons why children whine are discussed--because a child does not get his or her own way, because a child wants attention, because of boredom, because a child is tired or hungry, and so on. Alternatives to whining, such as talking things over with parents, resting, or finding something to do, are presented. How parents may deal with whining is also mentioned.

IL: Ages 4-6

3.14 Brandenberg. **Otto is Different.** see Ch. 8.

3.15 Brandenberg, Aliki. **Use Your Head, Dear.** New York: Greenwillow Books, 1983. 44 pp.

Charles the alligator seems to get everything mixed up at home and school--he falls asleep in the empty bathtub, goes out the window instead of the door, brushes his back with his toothbrush, paints the building blocks instead of on paper, etc. Exhausted with Charles's behavior, his mother asks Charles's father for advice. Unable to help his son remember by tying strings on his fingers and putting signs up all over the house, Charles's father finally gets results by giving Charles an invisible thinking cap.

IL: Ages 4-6

3.16 Brown, Marc and Stephen Krensky. **Perfect Pigs: An Introduction to Manners.** Boston: Little, Brown, and Company, 1983. 32 pp.

Young pigs are shown in a variety of situations trying to learn simple rules of etiquette to fit each situation. Good manners to use with one's family during mealtime, with one's pets, at parties, with friends, and at school are all illustrated and described in a humorous and relaxed style.

IL: Ages 4-6

3.17 Brown. **Someone Special, Just Like You.** see Ch. 10.

3.18 Caple. **The Biggest Nose.** see Ch. 8.

3.19 Carlson, Nancy. **Loudmouth George and the Fishing Trip.** Minneapolis: Carolrhoda Books, 1983. 28 pp.

George the rabbit boasts about all his activities and tells of catching a huge fish in the past. Therefore, he is reluctant to go on a fishing trip with his friend Harriet who soon discovers George knows nothing about fishing. George indeed catches a minnow-sized fish, yet when he starts to brag the next day, Harriet makes certain his story is correct.

IL: Ages 4-6

3.20 Cole, Joanna. **Aren't You Forgetting Something, Fiona?** New York: Parent's Magazine Press, 1983. 33 pp.

Everyone in Fiona the elephant's family has a good memory except Fiona, who frequently forgets items needed for school, etc. When Fiona signs up to take a class with a friend, she is afraid she will once again forget to attend. Each family member gives Fiona advice on how to remember her class and Fiona indeed finds her class with only one mishap.

IL: Ages 4-6

3.21 Corey, Dorothy. **Everybody Take Turns.** Chicago: Albert Whitman and Company, 1980. 29 pp.

Children are illustrated taking turns as they play, eat, go to the library, and so on. It is stressed that adults must take turns as well.

IL: Ages 2-6

3.22 Corey, Dorothy. **We All Share.** Chicago: Albert Whitman and Company, 1980. 30 pp.

Children are depicted sharing such things as pets, lunches, and toys. Sharing is shown to be reciprocal--when one shares, others are apt to be willing to share in return.

IL: Ages 2-6

3.23 Counsel, June. **But Martin!** Boston: Faber and Faber, 1984. 31 pp.

Four children dread their first day back at school until they meet Martin, an outer space creature. Each of the children has different colored skin and a different type of hair; they also have varying abilities for schoolwork. Martin, who has green skin and no hair, helps the children with math and spelling and makes it an enjoyable school day for all four children before he zooms off in his saucer.

IL: Ages 4-6

3.24 Crary, Elizabeth. **I Can't Wait.** Seattle: Parenting Press, 1982. 29 pp.

Finding it difficult to wait his turn for jumping on a mattress, Luke comes up with several ideas for solving his problem. In addition to playing with someone else or finding another activity, Luke considers pushing the other person off, fussing about it, and asking a grownup for help. The possible outcome for each of these solutions is discussed and the feelings associated with each action are illustrated.

IL: Ages 4-6

3.25 Crary. **I Want It.** see Ch. 7.

3.26 Crary, Elizabeth. **I Want to Play.** Seattle: Parenting Press, 1982. 29 pp.

Tired of playing alone, Danny considers several alternatives to get someone to play with him. He could wait for someone to ask him to play or disturb other children, both ideas which probably won't solve his problem. Other more positive solutions are explored as well, such as asking an adult for help and inviting someone to play with him.

IL: Ages 4-6

3.27 Crary. **My Name is not Dummy.** see Ch. 7.

3.28 Delton. **I'm Telling You Now.** see Ch. 4.

3.29 Dickinson, Mary. **Alex's Bed.** London: Andre Deutsch, 1980. 29 pp.

Alex claims his room is always such a mess because he doesn't have enough space for his belongings. In an effort to find a solution to

Alex's problem, his mother decides to build a bed on stilts, complete with a ladder and a safety rail. Sure enough Alex's room has more space when his new bed is completed; however, his mother discovers the problem is actually Alex, who likes to be messy.

IL: Ages 4-6

3.30 Dickinson. **Alex's Outing.** see Ch. 7.

3.31 Drescher, Joan. **The Marvelous Mess.** Boston: Houghton Mifflin, 1980. 30 pp.

Disturbed over their young son's terribly messy bedroom, his parents order him not to emerge from his room until it's cleaned. While his older sister makes snide comments and his parents worry about whether their punishment was too harsh, the boy rearranges his mess to create a circus, a pirate ship, a restaurant, etc. Right before his deadline, the boy crams everything into his closet. His parents are quite pleased with his seemingly neat room, but the boy's knowing older sister slams the door as she leaves causing the closet door to open.

IL: Ages 4-6

3.32 Drescher. **Your Family, My Family.** see Ch. 9.

3.33 Elliot, Dan. **Ernie's Little Lie.** New York: Random House, 1983. 32 pp.

In order to win a painting contest, Ernie enters a tiger picture made by his cousin. When everyone agrees that the tiger painting should win first prize, Ernie finds he cannot accept the prize and tells the truth about the situation. Ernie is congratulated for his honesty and the prize is to be sent to his cousin.

IL: Ages 4-6

3.34 Gambill, Henrietta. **Self-Control.** Chicago: Children's Press, 1982. 29 pp.

Self-control is defined as listening to someone else talk when you want to, letting someone else take the biggest piece of candy, being quiet in the library, waiting your turn, etc. Using self-control to get along better with siblings is also discussed. It is stated that thinking about and deciding what is right for you (self-control) will make one a happier person.

IL: Ages 4-6

3.35 Glass, Andrew. **My Brother Tries to Make Me Laugh.** New York: Lothrop, Lee, and Shepard, 1984. 28 pp.

Bored with their long journey, two space creatures who are brother and sister make up stories about the life they expect to find on earth. Once their spaceship lands, their mother cautions them to not poke fun at the strange looking earthlings. The outerspace children and the earthlings find they have much in common.

IL: Ages 4-6

3.36 Gretz, Susanna. **It's Your Turn, Roger!** New York: E.P. Dutton, 1985. 24 pp.

Unhappy about household chores he's asked to perform, Roger the pig stomps out of his house to eat with one of his neighbors. Roger visits several neighbor's homes where he is a guest and doesn't have to help out, but he doesn't care for any of the meals they're serving. Deciding his own home and family is the best, Roger heads home and promises to cheerfully set the table the next day.

IL: Ages 4-6

3.37 Guzzo. **Fox and Heggie.** see Ch. 7.

3.38 Harris, Robie. **I Hate Kisses.** New York: Alfred A. Knopf, 1981. 28 pp.

Peter decides he has outgrown being kissed and is too old to play with a stuffed dinosaur, which he replaces with a robot. He gives his dinosaur to his father with instructions on its care. He also hits his mother's arm to show how strong he is, but she claims she would have preferred a kiss. Only when Peter falls on his robot and hurts his knee, does he change his mind about kissing and request the return of his stuffed dinosaur.

IL: Ages 4-6

3.39 Hayes, Geoffrey. **Patrick Eats His Dinner.** New York: Alfred A. Knopf, 1985. 29 pp.

Four-year old Patrick claims that the peas on his dinner plate are poison. Patrick hides his peas in his napkin, but mother discovers them and gives him another helping. Finally Patrick mixes his peas with all the other food on his plate and finds that the new mixture is quite tasty.

IL: Ages 2-6

3.40 Hazen, Barbara. **Even if I Did Something Awful.** New York: Atheneum, 1981. 27 pp.

A little girl inquires whether her mother would still love her if she performed various misdeeds. The mother replies that she would always love her daughter; however, the little girl would need to clean up, be punished, etc. When the little girl admits to breaking her mother's favorite vase, the mother scolds her and makes her help clean up, yet she assures the little girl that she is still loved.

IL: Ages 4-6

3.41 Hazen. **It's a Shame about the Rain...** see Ch. 2.

3.42 Hurd, Edith. **I Dance in My Red Pajamas.** New York: Harper and Row, 1982. 28 pp.

Although her parents admonish her to have extra good behavior when she visits her grandparents, Jenny looks forward to her overnight stay. Jenny's grandparents don't care if she's noisy and they appreciate her help with all the chores. After a wonderful, active, noisy day, Jenny and her grandparents tiredly go upstairs to bed.

IL: Ages 4-6

3.43 Joosse, Barbara. **The Thinking Place.** New York: Alfred A. Knopf, 1982. 30 pp.

After she puts candy corn in the dishwasher, Elisabeth is sent by her mother to the thinking place. While there, Elisabeth considers other misbehavior in the past. She also imagines having a tea party with a friend, being chased by a gila monster, and being blamed for misdeeds a witch commits. After apologizing and making up with her mother, Elisabeth rushes back to her room to insure that her fantasy friends don't get her into any more trouble.

IL: Ages 4-6

3.44 Keller. **Cromwell's Glasses.** see Ch. 10.

3.45 Keller, Irene. **The Thingumajig Book of Manners.** Chicago: Children's Press, 1981. 28 pp.

The thingumajigs demonstrate all the "no-nos" of etiquette, including sloppy table manners, interrupting conversations, and poor sportsmanship. Two children illustrate the "good manners" alternative to each of the thingumajig's actions. This provides a humorous approach to discussions of manners.

IL: Ages 4-6

3.46 Kent, Jack. **Joey Runs Away.** Englewood Cliffs, NJ: Prentice-Hall, 1985. 28 pp.

Not wanting to clean his room within mother kangaroo's pocket, Joey decides to run away. Mother Kangaroo frantically searches for young Joey, while other animals in search of a home try to move into her pouch. Joey doesn't have much luck finding a new place to live either. He returns home in a mailman's pouch and happily starts cleaning up his room.

IL: Ages 4-6

3.47 Kline, Suzy. **Shhhh!** Chicago: Albert Whitman and Company, 1984. 28 pp.

A noisy, playful little girl is always being hushed by the grown-ups and older siblings in her family. She is reminded to be quiet at school, the library, and at church as well. After she goes outside and makes all the loud noises she can think of, the little girl doesn't mind so much being quiet when she's inside.

IL: Ages 2-6

3.48 Lindgren, Barbro. **The Wild Baby.** New York: Greenwillow Books, 1980. 21 pp.

Baby Ben seems determined to get into mischief; he climbs the chandelier, falls into the toilet, and swims in the sink. His mother scolds him with no results. Ben even runs away, but his mother always finds him and gladly takes him home.

IL: Ages 2-6

3.49 Lutrell. **Lonesome Lester.** see Ch. 2.

3.50 McNulty, Sally. **Learn with Moonbird: Manners.** Windermere, Florida: The Rourke Corporation, 1983. 31 pp.

Tired of Lizzie's lack of consideration for others, Lizzie's parents ask her to live in their barn. There Lizzie meets Moonbird who takes her to another planet where everyone has poor manners. After watching the extra-terrestrial beings, Lizzie becomes exasperated with their lack of knowledge of the simple rules of etiquette. Moonbird returns Lizzie to her home where she apologizes to her parents and starts making a list of good manners she feels are important.

IL: Ages 4-6

3.51 McPhail, David. **Alligators Are Awful (and they have terrible manners too).** Garden City, NY: Doubleday and Company, 1980. 31 pp.

A little girl claims that alligators are awful and proceeds to list examples of their poor manners. She claims they are rude when asked a question, block other's views at the movies, push at the bus stop, can't keep a secret, and break other's toys. After mentioning their terrible table manners and telephone habits as well, the little girl exclaims that she is glad people don't act like those awful alligators.

IL: Ages 4-6

3.52 Malloy, Judy. **Bad Thad.** New York: E.P. Dutton, 1980. 28 pp.

Thad starts the day off misbehaving--he won't get ready for preschool, disobeys the rules once he's there, and feeds his lunch to the dog and won't nap at home. He won't cooperate during his checkup with the doctor, causes a disturbance at the library, and creates havoc at two stores as well. Although getting Thad ready for bed is not easy either, his exhausted parents lovingly tuck him into bed.

IL: Ages 2-4

3.53 Meddaugh, Susan. **Beast.** Boston: Houghton Mifflin, 1981. 32 pp.

After Anna spots a beast in the forest, her parents and siblings declare it must be bad, dangerous, strong, and ferocious despite the fact that they have never seen it. Brave Anna decides to find out about the beast herself and proceeds to feed the beast and warn it that it's in danger. Discovering that the beast is actually fearful and very meek, Anna releases the beast so that it is protected from the others.

IL: Ages 4-6

3.54 Moncure, Jane. **Saying Please.** Chicago: Children's Press, 1982. 29 pp.

Various situations where the word "please" should be used are described--when a child needs help from an adult or peer, when a child wants something passed at the table, when a child wants someone to share an activity, etc. The advantages of using "please" when making a request are also stressed.

IL: Ages 4-6

3.55 Mueller, Virginia. **A Playhouse for Monster.** Chicago: Albert Whitman and Company, 1985. 21 pp.

Very possessive of his playhouse, Monster makes a "Keep Out" sign when another monster approaches. Monster finds that having a snack alone inside his playhouse is not much fun. He therefore prepares a second snack and makes a new sign saying "Welcome."

IL: Ages 2-4

3.56 Newfield, Marcia. **Where Did You Put Your Sleep?** New York: Atheneum, 1983. 24 pp.

Trying to avoid going to sleep each night, Annie comes up with a number of reasons for getting out of bed; she needs a drink, has to use the bathroom, hears funny sounds, etc. Annie's mother begins to lose patience with her daughter. However, Annie's father invents a game where he and Annie search for her sleep, with the result that Annie relaxes and does fall asleep.

IL: Ages 2-6

3.57 O'Brien, Anne. **I Want That!** New York: Holt, Rinehart, and Winston, 1985. 14 pp.

Deciding she wants the toy younger Nicholas is playing with, Meagan grabs it away and starts playing with it herself. She feels bad though when Nicholas cries and Meagan returns the toy, suggesting that they try to share it.

IL: Ages 2-4

3.58 Oxenbury. **The Birthday Party.** see Ch. 7.

3.59 Oxenbury, Helen. **Eating Out.** New York: E.P. Dutton, 1983. 16 pp.

A toddler finds his first meal at a restaurant with his parents to be quite boring. It is difficult to wait for his food and he doesn't please his mother when he requests a trip to the bathroom. After he causes a waiter with a tray of food to trip, the little boy's parents leave the restaurant for home, where the child preferred to be anyway.

IL: Ages 2-4

3.60 Panek, Dennis. **Matilda Hippo Has a Big Mouth.** Scarsdale, NY: Bradbury Press, 1980. 29 pp.

After making thoughtless remarks about her friends' physical appearances, Matilda Hippo can't understand why her peers shun her. Some unkind graffiti written about her upsets Matilda even more. Matilda and her friends call a truce, with the result that hopefully Matilda will think first before she speaks.

IL: Ages 4-6

3.61 Parish. **I Can-Can You?** (Level 4). see Ch. 8.

3.62 Porter, David. **Mine!** Boston: Houghton Mifflin, 1981. 32 pp.

A little boy cries and sulks whenever he wants something. However, as soon as he obtains that object, he quickly discards it and wails for something else. When he finally finds himself alone with nothing left to want, the little boy starts to think about things in terms of "our" rather than always "mine."

IL: Ages 2-4

3.63 Quackenbush, Robert. **I Don't Want to Go, I Don't Know How to Act.** New York: J.B. Lippincott, 1983. 29 pp.

A young bear avoids going to restaurants and parties with his parents because he is convinced he won't have good behavior at such places. When the bear's uncle asks the family to meet him for dinner and a sitter is unavailable, the little bear is quite nervous. His mother, however, coaches the little bear in the basics of polite conversation and the dinner is a success.

IL: Ages 4-6

3.64 Rabe. **The Balancing Girl.** see Ch. 10.

3.65 Reece, Colleen. **Saying Thank You.** Chicago: Children's Press, 1982. 29 pp.

When a friend shares something, when parents plan something special, when a child just enjoys being with someone--these are all appropriate times for a child to say "thank you." The positive reaction of others to the words "thank you" is also mentioned.

IL: Ages 4-6

3.66 Rockwell. **Can I Help?** see Ch. 4.

3.67 Rogers. **Going to Day Care.** see Ch. 7.

3.68 Rosenberg. **My Friend Leslie...** see Ch. 10.

3.69 Ross, Tony. **Naughty Nicky.** New York: Holt, Rinehart, and Winston, 1982. 23 pp.

To avoid doing chores, Nicky spends a week pretending to misunderstand his parents' requests for help--he washes the fishes instead of the dishes, etc. During a dream about a little man who will grant him wishes, Nicky is horrified when the little man mixes up each wish. Nicky awakens from the nightmare and decides perhaps he shouldn't continue his naughty misinterpretations.

IL: Ages 4-6

3.70 Sadler, Marilyn. **The Very Bad Bunny.** New York: Random House, 1984. 38 pp.

The Funnybunny family thinks P.J. is "bad" when he is involved in an occasional mishap around the house. Then P.J.'s cousin Binky arrives for a visit; he ruins toys, wrecks the furniture, and locks everyone out of the house. After comparing Binky's behavior to P.J.'s, the Funnybunny family decides P.J. is not such a bad bunny after all.

IL: Ages 2-6

3.71 Sarnoff, Jane and Reynold Ruffins. **That's Not Fair.** New York: Charles Scribner's Sons, 1980. 28 pp.

Becky's favorite expression is "That's not fair!" when she has nothing to do, when she has to clean her room, when everyone is too busy to play with her. Older brother Bert explains "fairness" in terms of dividing chocolate cake into pieces and elephants being the only animal to have four knees. Becky then uses this definition to determine whether family happenings are indeed fair or not.

IL: Ages 4-6

3.72 Scarry, Richard. **Pig Will and Pig Won't.** New York: Random House, 1984. 19 pp.

Two brothers, Pig Will and Pig Won't, depict good and awful manners. Pig Will helps with chores, eats carefully, goes to bed when told, shares his toys, etc. and appears to be happy and well-liked. Pig Won't balks at every parental request and subsequently seems to be miserable and miss out on a lot of good times. Pig Won't finally decides to use "please" and "thank you" and to cooperate with his parents on a trial basis and soon the brothers are known as Pig Will and Me Too.

IL: Ages 4-6

3.73 Sharmat, Marjorie. **Bartholomew the Bossy.** New York: Macmillan, 1984. 32 pp.

When popular Bartholomew Skunk is elected president of a club, he starts telling all his friends what to do. Tired of being bossed, Bartholomew's friends avoid him and he feels very disliked and lonely. Upon the advice of his wise owl friend, Bartholomew stops bossing everyone and becomes a more reasonable club president.

IL: Ages 4-6

3.74 Sharmat. **Come Home, Wilma.** see Ch. 5.

3.75 Sharmat. **Rollo and Juliet, Forever!** see Ch. 7.

3.76 Sharmat. **Taking Care of Melvin.** see Ch. 7.

3.77 Simon. **Nobody's Perfect, Not Even My Mother.** see Ch. 8.

3.78 Stadler, John. **Gorman and the Treasure Chest.** Scarsdale, NY: Bradbury Press, 1984. 27 pp.

During a fishing expedition, Gorman the pig falls into a lake where he discovers a treasure chest. The chest is seized by a turtle, then a bear, and finally by a group of animal pirates. However, Gorman is the only one who can unlock the chest and he refuses to do so until everyone grudgingly agrees to share its contents.

IL: Ages 4-6

3.79 Ward, Nick. **Giant.** New York: Oxford University Press, 1982. 22 pp.

A giant sized girl who is bored has fun pushing over buildings and ruining the surrounding countryside. She feels totally in control until her father appears at the bedroom door and surveys the mess in her room. The little girl, who appeared to be a giant compared to her toy buildings, quickly cleans up her room so that she may have tea.

IL: Ages 2-6

3.80 Watson. **Jamie's Story.** see Ch. 4.

3.81 Winthrop. **Katharine's Doll.** see Ch. 7.

3.82 Wood, Audrey. **Tugford Wanted to be Bad.** New York: Harcourt Brace Jovanovich, 1983. 30 pp.

Tugford the mouse's favorite game is playing outlaw. When he decides to stop pretending and actually be an outlaw, he takes something from his parents' room and buries it in the yard. Unable to lie about his deed, Tugford asks his parents' help in searching for the stolen object, only to discover it was a present for him.

IL: Ages 4-6

3.83 Wylie, Joanne and David. **Have You Hugged Your Monster Today?** Chicago: Children's Press, 1984. 32 pp.

Good manners are demonstrated by a monster who covers its face when sneezing, eats carefully, hangs up its coat, and so on. The monster also helps its friends, shares, listens to others, and cleans up toys. In short, the monster personifies many positive traits for children to imitate.

IL: Ages 4-6

3.84 Ziefert, Harriet. **clappity clap!** New York: Viking Press, 1984. 14 pp.

A boy and girl share in activities such as building with blocks, pretend cooking, and dancing as well as sharing secrets and cookies.

IL: Ages 2-4

3.85 Ziefert. **zippety zip!** see Ch. 8.

4

Family Relationships

Clearly the family system has an important impact on a child's development. A child's interactions and experiences with family members provide a foundation for the lifelong process of socialization. Parents have a tendency to interact with their children in a fairly predictable way. These interactional patternings can have an impact on a child's development. There are also a number of patternings of interaction that have been identified between siblings, which impact a child's development as well.

Types of Parenting Interaction

Child development specialists have long searched for ingredients of parenting that would promote competent emotional and social development in children. In the 1930s John Watson, for example, argued that parents were too affectionate toward their children(1). Currently developmental specialists would largely disagree with Watson's position. In fact, many theorists and researchers feel that large numbers of children are starved for affection, given the changing nature of the family.

Diana Baumrind has studied in detail current types of parent-child interaction in families(2). Her research has focused on the control-autonomy dimension of parenting in the modern family. She has subdivided the control-autonomy dimension into psychological control-psychological autonomy and firm control-lax control. Psychological control consists of parental behavior that keeps the child closely tied to the parent, while psychological autonomy refers to parental behavior that allows the child more freedom and independence. The parent using firm control sets rules and regulations and requires the child to abide by them, while lax control results when the parent establishes rules but does not enforce them.

Baumrind reports that a high degree of psychological control promotes dependent, regressive behavior, for example crying and thumbsucking or difficulty in establishing peer relationships. Extensive control of the child's activities may also inhibit the child and contribute to shy behavior. However, the parent who uses lax control may encourage impulsive behavior in a child. Baumrind concludes that competent parenting is characterized by behavior that is neither excessively high nor low in control. Her research supports the belief that parents should be neither punitive toward their children nor aloof from them, but rather should develop rules for their children and enforce them.

Baumrind suggests that there are three types of parenting that impact a child's development: authoritarian, authoritative, and laissez-faire. A number of characteristics in children have been identified with each form of parenting.

Authoritarian parenting. Parents who are restrictive and punitive fall under this category of parenting. The parent typically allows little give and take with the child and places many limits on the child. This type of parenting is linked with children who show high levels of anxiety, ineffective social interaction with others, and underdevelopment socially in a number of key areas.

Authoritative parenting. This kind of parenting encourages independence; however it places limits, demands, and control on a child's actions. There is much verbal give-and-take, and parents demonstrate a high degree of warmth and support toward the child. Children who experience this type of parenting often will show greater social competency, self-reliance and social responsibility.

Laissez-faire parenting. When parents use this style of parenting they place low demands, limits, and controls on the child's behavior. This parenting style gives children considerable freedom to regulate their own behavior, with parents taking a nonpunitive stance. The parent using a laissez-faire style is not very involved with the child. Children raised under this kind of parenting style have a tendency to be immature, regressive, and unable to assume leadership positions.

Baumrind concludes that the most significant distinction is between authoritarian and authoritative parenting. A number of developmental specialists have argued that one style is superior to the other. Even though the debate is far from clear in regard to these two parenting styles, a controlling but warm approach to parenting appears to be more effective. Consequently, authoritative parenting would appear to be superior to an authoritarian approach to parenting.

One of the limitations of the literature on parent-child interaction has been that most of the research focuses on mother and child. In fact, parenting has been largely equated with mothering(3). Fathers have been generally viewed as merely an economic factor in family life and not psychologically important to family functioning. John Bowlby has suggested that the father is of no direct importance to young children, but is only of indirect value as economic support and in his emotional support of the mother(4). Margaret Mead has even referred to the father as a biological necessity, but a social accident(5). Fortunately recent literature published over the last few years has focused more on fathering. For example, it was recently found in a survey of two major journals on the family that father and mother as a dyad impacting children were studied more often than only mother-child interaction in the literature(6). Clearly both parents play a vital role in the growth and development of children; currently more emphasis is being placed on the role of fathers in this process.

Over the last several decades there has been a major change in how parents view and interact with children. Not long ago it was felt that the most effective way to deal with children was to meet force with force. For example, if a preschool child threw a temper tantrum the child should be punished. However, today parents deal with the problem of temper tantrums by not reinforcing such behavior through not responding to it or possibly by attempting to teach the child more socially acceptable ways of expressing anger. It is common knowledge that children are naturally curious about their environment. The three-year-old child can try a parent's patience with numerous questions in trying to make sense out of the world. It is generally felt that parental responding to such curiosity is quite important for developing a child's intellect. Many parents now realize in their interaction with children that love and hate are counterparts to each other. A preschool child may have these feelings of love and hate so confused that the child might say, "I love you so much that I hate you."

Informed parents as well as professionals who work with children realize that growth and development are a complex process that is predictable in many ways. The way parents interact with their children and the ways that families interact as a system have critical consequences on the development of children. There are clearly ways in which parents approach their children that can support and nurture their development.

Sibling Relations

A child's siblings are some of the most important individuals influencing a child's development. Siblings must learn to cooperate with each other and to share such things as love, possessions, and physical space. They must also learn to adapt to each other; this process impacts how a child deals with the family system as well as with people outside the family.

The phenomenon of sibling rivalry is one of the key issues when one tries to understand problems related to sibling interaction. When a child is confronted with a newborn and assumes the role of older brother or sister, a whole set of feelings and emotions occur at once, including jealousy, anger, and so on. The extent of sibling rivalry is related to the age of the firstborn. A preschool child who is twenty months of age when confronted with a new sibling may not be as difficult to deal with as a four- or five-year-old child. The older preschool child may well break or hide the toys of a newborn whereas the child of twenty months is not likely to behave in such an aggressive manner.

If the preschool child has already established a number of contacts outside the family system through day-care or playmates, the arrival of a newborn may not be as threatening to the child(7). Regardless if this is the case or not, jealousy will still exist in the older child. In fact a parent may not recognize the jealousy because it may be very subtle. An example might be the child who hugs the new brother or sister so hard that the baby cries. Children, typically in the early-childhood stage of development, show their anger and hostility toward a new sibling in a very direct fashion such as hitting and crying about having a new family member. Parents can prepare the preschool child for the impending birth by exposing the child to newborns, moving the child to a new room or new bed well in advance of the baby's arrival, and insuring that individual parental time is scheduled for the firstborn after the baby's arrival.

The aspect that is particularly critical about sibling interaction is that children learn how to share parental time and how to share with each other. Learning to share with other family members is a very good teaching process for learning how to deal with the world outside the family. Parents should play a role in the managing of sibling interaction, while trying not to take sides, to insure the quality of the interaction. In fact, it can be very beneficial to children if a parent sets time aside each day to join in the play of their children.

The literature also suggests that family size may have a real impact on the importance of sibling interaction to children. Obviously in large families, children must learn to share physical space and parental time much differently than in smaller family systems. Siblings should have their own turf; this may be drawers, shelves, or toys that are designated exclusive property of each child. Each child is different and comparisons between siblings should be avoided. One very effective way parents in large families can improve their interaction time with children is through planned group activities. Clearly a number of problems and issues are likely to exist in sibling relationships; many of these are fairly predictable and can be dealt with effectively by a parent or professional person.

The Family in Early Childhood Literature

Young children take pleasure in seeing the familiar relationships of home reflected in their books, whether the characters are human or animals(8). Many books for children this age deal with a child's relationship with the mother as she nurtures the child and teaches the first lessons about loving and caring. More and more books for the preschool child examine life with father as well, often when the mother is absent from the home because of work. Fathers are shown as being capable of managing the household and child care as well as mothers. The family is portrayed as a unit that works and plays together, as a refuge of love and security where the first lessons about getting along with others are learned.

All families have their problems, though, and these circumstances are a part of certain children's books as well. A child in a book may feel put upon because parents expect a small show of responsibility, such as making a bed. Other book characters want to help out and to feel needed, but other family members are too busy to accomodate them. A very trying part of the day for families may involve a child's bath and bedtime; humorous and fairly predictable ways that parents deal with this problem are depicted in various books for the preschool child.

The arrival of a new sibling is a very significant event in a young child's life and the child's typical feelings of jealousy and abandonment by parents are the theme of many books for preschool children. Sibling problems do not go away once the baby grows up either. Early-childhood books dealing with the difficulties in sharing possessions, arguing over trivial household matters, and vying for parental attention all hit a realistic note. Another important need among siblings, especially felt by twins and triplets, is the desire to establish a separate place for oneself slightly distant from the family but within easy reach of its affectionate reassurance(9).

Responses to the literature. Stories about family relationships should prove reassuring to any young child. Children, as well as their parents, may identify themselves in books concerning family life. The child will likely see a book character coping with the tasks of becoming a sharing and responsible family member. Parents reading aloud to a child may encourage laughter and discussion about the solutions to bedtime, bath hassles, etc. that mothers and fathers in the books come up with.

The adult guide utilizing literature to meet the needs of a preschool child concerning family relationships can augment discussion of the book with various follow-up activities. With consideration of the child's age and abilities, the helper could work with the child(ren) on activities such as the following:

1. Creating a family mobile with photographs or pictures drawn by the child.

2. Constructing the child's family tree in very simple form, going back perhaps as far as grandparents.

3. Listing the advantages and disadvantages of being a younger or older sibling.

4. Making clay figures or constructing puppets to represent family members, followed by dramatization of a story event.

5. Writing a short story dictated by the child on some aspect of family life, such as helping father prepare breakfast, playing with a baby brother or sister, or a family outing(10).

Since the relationships developed within the family will influence preschool children in later years as they make friends and cope with school, being read stories about various aspects of family life would seem suitable for all preschool children. The child's physical, social, and emotional development are all rooted in the child's family; thus literature about family life definitely fulfills a developmental need. Especially when supplemented by a follow-up activity, early-childhood books concerning relationships with parents or siblings can provoke positive involvement in the child's exploration of developmental needs.

NOTES

1. John W. Santrock and Steven R. Yussen, **Children and Adolescents-A Developmental Perspective** (Dubuque, Iowa: William C. Brown, 1984), p. 214.

2. Diana Baumrind, "Current Patterns of Parental Authority," **Developmental Psychology Monographs** (Volume IV, 1971): 1.

3. Julius Segal and Herbert Yahraes, **A Child's Journey** (New York: McGraw-Hill, 1979), p. 105.

4. John Bowlby, **Maternal Care and Mental Health** Monograph Series, No. 2 (Geneva: World Health Organization, 1951).

5. Margaret Mead, "A Cultural Anthropologist's Approach to Maternal Deprivation," in **Deprivation of Maternal Care: A Reassessment of Its Effects** (Geneva: World Health Organization, 1962).

6. E.E. LeMaster and John DeFrain, **Parents in Contemporary America—A Sympathetic View** (Homewood, Illinois: The Dorsey Press, 1983), pp. 153-154.

7. Elizabeth B. Hurlock, **Child Development** 6th ed. (New York: McGraw-Hill, 1978), p. 65.

8. Zena Sutherland, Dianne Monson, and May Hill Arbuthnot, **Children and Books** 6th ed. (Glenview, Illinois: Scott, Foresman and Company, 1981), p. 106.

9. Myra Sadker and David Sadker, **Now Upon a Time: A Contemporary View of Children's Literature** (New York: Harper and Row, 1977), p. 19.

10. Margaret C. Gillespie and John W. Conner, **Creative Growth through Literature for Children and Adolescents** (Columbus, Ohio: Charles E. Merrill, 1975); Jean A. Pardeck and John T. Pardeck, **Young People with Problems: A Guide to Bibliotherapy** (Westport, Connecticut: Greenwood Press, 1984); Ellen Weiss, **Sesame Street—My Memory Book** (New York: Children's Television Workshop, 1983).

BOOKS

4.1 Alda. **Sonya's Mommy Works.** see Ch. 8.

4.2 Alexander, Martha. **When the New Baby Comes, I'm Moving Out.** New York: The Dial Press, 1981. 32 pp.

Upset over his mother's preparation for the arrival of a new sibling, Oliver claims he is running away. He also makes plans to take his mother and the new baby to the city dump, once it arrives. However, when Oliver's mother describes the special privileges big brothers are entitled to and how much she needs him, Oliver starts to eagerly anticipate his new sibling's arrival.

IL: Ages 2-6

4.3 Armitage. **The Bossing of Josie.** see Ch. 2.

4.4 Asch. **Goodnight Horsey.** see Ch. 8.

4.5 Banish, Roslyn. **I Want to Tell You About My Baby.** Berkeley: Wingbow Press, 1982. 46 pp.

A small boy is excited about his mother's pregnancy and making preparations for the new baby, yet he wishes his mother wasn't so tired all the time. His grandparents arrive to take care of him and he goes to the hospital to visit his mother and the new baby. Although he helps his mother with the baby at home, the little boy resents the baby's crying and his having to play quietly when the baby naps. The parents insure that the little boy still feels loved and receives plenty of attention from them.

IL: Ages 4-6

4.6 Bauer. **My Mom Travels a Lot.** see Ch. 8.

4.7 Berenstain. **The Berenstain Bears and Mama's New Job.** see Ch. 8.

4.8 Berenstain. **The Berenstain Bears and the Messy Room.** see Ch. 3.

4.9 Berenstain, Stan and Jan. **The Berenstain Bears Get in a Fight.** New York: Random House, 1982. 29 pp.

When Brother and Sister Bear start the day with a fight, their inability to get along grows into a heated argument by evening. The two siblings refuse to speak to one another, won't play together, take away toys, etc. Mama Bear compares their arguing to the storm outside and urges them to make up when a rainbow appears at the storm's end.

IL: Ages 4-6

4.10 Bond, Felicia. **Poinsettia and Her Family.** New York: Thomas Y. Crowell, 1981. 32 pp.

Although she loves their big old house, Poinsettia Pig feels it is too crowded with six sisters and brothers always in the way. After a day of misbehavior directed toward her many siblings, Poinsettia is relieved when the rest of her family goes on a search for a larger home. Poinsettia revels in having the quiet house all to herself, but when evening comes, she grows lonely and is happy to see her noisy, happy family returning home.

IL: Ages 4-6

4.11 Brennan, Jan. **Born Two-gether.** Avon, CT: J and L Books, 1984, 35 pp.

The difference between identical twins and fraternal twins is simply explained. Along with problems faced by many siblings (being compared to one another, sharing a bedroom, sharing their parents), the unique stresses twins face are discussed as well--identical twins being mistaken for one another, being known as "the twins" rather than as individuals, having to share a birthday. However, there are many joys involved with being a twin and the camaraderie they share makes twinship a special experience.

IL: Ages 2-6

4.12 Carlson, Nancy. **Harriet and Walt.** Minneapolis: Carolrhoda Books, 1982. 28 pp.

Harriet is excited about playing in the newly fallen snow until her mother reminds Harriet that her little brother must accompany her. Little brother Walt manages to ruin Harriet's snow tunnel, knocks down their snowman, and is unable to make a snow angel. Harriet becomes quite disgusted with Walt until a playmate her age starts to criticize him as well. Then Harriet comes to the rescue and decides to educate her little brother on how to have fun in the snow.

IL: Ages 4-6

4.13 Chorao. **Kate's Quilt.** see Ch. 2.

4.14 Cole, Joanna. **The New Baby at Your House.** New York: William Morrow and Company, 1985. 48 pp.

Young children are shown with their pregnant mothers, and later at the hospital visiting their mothers and new siblings. Ways that older siblings can assist such as entertaining the baby and helping to change diapers are stressed. Negative feelings are also explored--an older child's anger at the baby's crying, jealousy at the attention the baby receives, and perhaps even wishing the baby could be returned. Most importantly, individual differences between siblings are discussed and the family unit is portrayed as having enough love for all members.

IL: Ages 4-6

4.15 Corey. **New Shoes.** see Ch. 2.

4.16 Delton, Judy. **I'm Telling You Now**. New York: E.P. Dutton, 1983. 28 pp.

When Artie's mother scolds him for climbing a ladder, going to a party uninvited, and walking a strange dog, Artie claims he didn't realize he was not supposed to do these things. As Artie comes to the realization that his mother doesn't approve of certain behavior, he decides to check with her before embarking on his next adventure.

IL: Ages 4-6

4.17 Dickinson. **Alex's Outing**. see Ch. 7.

4.18 Dickinson, Mike. **My Brother's Silly**. London: Andre Deutsch, 1983. 26 pp.

While mother works on the weekends, dad and his two sons spend an eventful day at home and at the park. To dad's chagrin, the youngest brother seems to always be in trouble and likes to imagine he is such things as a postcard, hat, dog, soccer ball, etc. Although dad is quite worn out by evening, he and older brother do dishes while mom puts little brother to bed.

IL: Ages 4-6

4.19 Dragonwagon, Crescent. **I Hate My Brother Harry**. New York: Harper and Row, 1983. 32 pp.

A young girl claims that she hates her much older brother because he embarrasses her, doesn't share, teases her, etc. However, she also recalls many fun times with Harry. Although her mother claims they will one day be friends, the little girl continues to have mixed feelings about her brother.

IL: Ages 4-6

4.20 Drescher. **Your Family, My Family**. see Ch. 9.

4.21 Edelman, Elaine. **I Love My Baby Sister (Most of the Time)**. New York: Lothrop, Lee, and Shepard, 1984. 22 pp.

A toddler girl likes to sing to, cuddle, and make funny noises with her baby sister. She doesn't like the baby yanking her hair, grabbing her nose, and screaming. Most of all, the little girl looks forward to her baby sister getting older so they can share many activities together.

IL: Ages 2-4

4.22 Frankel, Alona. **The Family of Tiny White Elephants**. Woodbury, NY: Barron's, 1980. 36 pp.

A boy elephant has a near perfect life in the jungle with his parents until a baby sister arrives. Then the young elephant feels neglected and considers regressing in his behavior to receive equal attention from his mother and father. Only when brother elephant tells his parents about his anger and his wish to return the baby sister, do his parents express their love for him and make an effort to spend more time in his favorite activities.

IL: Ages 4-6

4.23 Galbraith, Kathryn. **Katie Did!** New York: Atheneum, 1982. 27 pp.

After being scolded for dancing and singing while her baby brother tries to sleep, Mary Rose attempts to help her mother by pouring her own juice and preparing the baby's bath. When her mother finally gets the baby to sleep and asks Mary Rose about all the mess, Mary Rose claims her doll did it all and should be thrown away. Mama takes time out to rock Mary Rose and reassure her that she is loved; then they both head for the sandpile to play.

IL: Ages 2-4

4.24 Glass. **My Brother Tries to Make Me Laugh.** see Ch. 3.

4.25 Greydanus, Rose. **Double Trouble.** Mahwah, NJ: Troll Associates, 1981. 28 pp.

Twin raccoons Tim and Jim look alike, talk alike, and sometimes act alike. When good deeds are done, Tim and Jim both try to take credit for them; however, when mother discovers that someone has been mischievous, neither brother will take the blame.

IL: Ages 4-6

4.26 Hamilton, Morse. **Big Sisters are Bad Witches.** New York: Greenwillow Books, 1981. 29 pp.

Kate plans to treat her anticipated baby brother much better than older sister Emily treats her. When Kate and Emily scuffle in their father's study and a statue gets broken, both girls are angry with each other and dread their father's return home. However, father has news that their new sibling is indeed a boy and announces that Kate must learn to be a big sister as well as a little sister now.

IL: Ages 4-6

4.27 Hamilton-Merritt, Jane. **Our New Baby.** New York: Julian Messner, 1982. 24 pp.

Michael eagerly tells his friends about his mother's pregnancy. He and his older sister are allowed to visit the newborn in the hospital and help their parents with the baby once it is home. Michael's friend, who has an older baby brother, gives Michael advice on how to make babies laugh and to play carefully with them. Michael decides babies can be good friends.

IL: Ages 4-6

4.28 Hazen. **Even if I Did Something Awful.** see Ch. 3.

4.29 Hazen. **It's a Shame about the Rain...** see Ch. 2.

4.30 Henkes, Kevin. **Margaret and Taylor.** New York: Greenwillow Books, 1983. 64 pp.

Older sister Margaret is able to boss her younger brother and talk him into doing things she doesn't care to do herself. Young Taylor is more thoughtful of others and enjoys being with his sister anyway. During one of their sibling squabbles, their grandfather appears and is able to make peace between the brother and sister.

IL: Ages 4-6

4.31 Herman, Charlotte. **My Mother Didn't Kiss Me Good-Night.** New York: E.P. Dutton, 1980. 27 pp.

When his mother forgets to kiss him good-night, a young boy tries to figure out the reason why. After recalling various incidents during the day when he was naughty, the boy convinces himself that he doesn't need to be kissed anyway. Yet he is relieved when his mother comes to his room and explains why she didn't kiss him--she has a cold.

IL: Ages 4-6

4.32 Herold, Ann. **The Helping Day.** New York: Coward, McCann, and Geoghegan, 1980. 28 pp.

When various family members don't seem to need young David's help with their tasks, he goes outside and tries to think of something to do. David discovers he is capable of helping some ants, a worm, a butterfly caught in a spider web, and a baby rabbit. Tired with all his helpfulness, David proudly describes to his father all he has done that day.

IL: Ages 4-6

4.33 Hines, Anna. **Maybe a Band-Aid Will Help.** New York: E.P. Dutton, 1984. 22 pp.

When her doll loses a leg, Sarah is anxious for her mother to fix it, but Sarah's mother seems to be too busy that day. The next day is a disaster as Sarah and her friends unsuccessfully try to lessen her mother's household chores. Banished to her room, Sarah tries to mend the doll herself until her mother apologizes and takes time out to play hospital with Sarah and repair her doll.

IL: Ages 4-6

4.34 Hoban, Lillian. **No, No, Sammy Crow.** New York: Greenwillow Books, 1981. 29 pp.

Sammy Crow is scolded for sucking his thumb and carrying around a blanket. He and his older sister frequently quarrel; however, when the Robin brothers pick on Sammy, his older sister comes to his rescue. Sammy's mother praises her two children for working together and is pleased when Sammy gives up his blanket to warm his mother's newest egg.

IL: Ages 4-6

4.35 Hoffman, Rosekrans. **Sister Sweet Ella.** New York: William Morrow and Company, 1982. 27 pp.

Upset by all the attention his baby sister receives, Wadsworth decides to use magic to turn her into a cat, an animal his mother hates. When a scraggly cat does appear, Wadsworth unsuccessfully tries to find a home for it. His mother is so busy searching for the baby, she still can't pay attention to him. Simultaneously the cat disappears and the baby reappears with Wadsworth deciding to give up magic—maybe a baby sister isn't so bad after all.

IL: Ages 4-6

4.36 Hoopes. **When I Was Little.** see Ch. 6.

4.37 Hutchins, Pat. **The Very Worst Monster.** New York: Greenwillow Books, 1985. 27 pp.

Hazel Monster's baby brother has such awful, monstrous behavior that her parents are thrilled and seem not to notice Hazel anymore. Hazel's brother even manages to win the Worst Monster Baby contest, much to Hazel's chagrin. To prove what a monster she can be, Hazel gives away her baby brother, only to have him given back.

IL: Ages 4-6

4.38 Joosse. **The Thinking Place.** see Ch. 3.

4.39 Keller, Holly. **Too Big.** New York: Greenwillow Books, 1983. 29 pp.

When his parents bring home his new baby brother, Henry the possum is very unhappy. Everyone tells him he is "too big" to fit in the baby's bed, to drink out of a bottle, to wear a diaper, etc. When Henry tries on the baby's clothes, he has to admit he's too big for them; however, he's not too big for a hug from mother and a tricycle from his grandfather.

IL: Ages 2-4

4.40 Kempler. **A Man Can Be...** see Ch. 8.

4.41 Kline. **Shhhh!** see Ch. 3.

4.42 Lakin, Patricia. **Don't Touch My Room.** Boston: Little, Brown and Company, 1985. 32 pp.

Pleased with the familiarity of his room, Aaron is horrified with his parents' plans to remodel it to make space for a soon-to-be-born sibling. Aaron's possessions are packed away and he sleeps in the living room while workmen take over his bedroom. Although he is at first bored and later annoyed with his new baby brother, Aaron appreciates a secret spot in the bedroom made just for him. When baby brother is a little older and gets into mischief, Aaron even takes his sibling to the secret place to get away from their parents' angry words.

IL: Ages 4-6

4.43 Lasker, Joe. **The Do-Something Day.** New York: The Viking Press, 1982. 30 pp.

After both his parents and his older brother decline Bernie's offers to help, Bernie decides to run away. Wandering through his neighborhood, Bernie finds that the familiar storekeepers all need some help. Bernie returns home to his worried family who promise not to be so busy and declare they will ask more often for Bernie's assistance.

IL: Ages 4-6

4.44 Lasky, Kathryn. **A Baby for Max.** New York: Charles Scribner's Sons, 1984. 48 pp.

Four-year old Max is well prepared for the arrival of a new sibling--he accompanies his mother on her visits to the doctor, he attends a class on baby care, and he helps his parents make room for the baby at home. Although he likes his babysitter and gets to visit his mom and the baby at the hospital, Max is sad about the change in his routine. Max considers running away once the baby is home, but his mother reassures him that he received just as much attention and care when he was a baby.

IL: Ages 4-6

4.45 Lindgren, Astrid. **I Want a Brother or Sister.** New York: Harcourt, Brace, Jovanovich, 1981. 28 pp.

Young Peter asks his mother for a brother or sister and is surprised when his obviously pregnant mother tells him he will have a new sibling soon. Although Peter is initially fascinated with his baby sister, he soon grows jealous of her, acts disruptive, and thinks about trading her for a 3-wheeler. Mother assures Peter that he is still loved and asks him for help with the baby. Several years later, when a third child arrives, Peter is glad he has a sister to play with so neither is jealous of the baby.

IL: Ages 4-6

4.46 Lindgren. **The Wild Baby.** see Ch. 3.

4.47 Lloyd, Errol. **Nandy's Bedtime.** London: The Bodley Head, 1982. 24 pp.

Nandy, a young black girl, helps her mother pick up toys and cook dinner. After daddy assists Nandy with her bath and putting on pajamas, both parents tuck her into bed.

IL: Ages 2-4

4.48 McDaniel, Becky. **Katie Did It.** Chicago: Children's Press, 1983. 30 pp.

Katie, the youngest of three children, gets blamed for the spilled milk, toys left outside, the door being open, etc. She grows weary of always hearing her siblings say, "Katie did it." When she picks a bouquet of flowers for her mother, however, Katie is happy to take the credit for that deed.

IL: Ages 2-4

4.49 McPhail, David. **Sisters.** New York: Harcourt Brace Jovanovich, 1984. 26 pp.

Two sisters share a love of horses, skating, dancing, and drawing. However, they realize their many differences in food preference, dressing, sleeping habits, etc. Most importantly, they have fun together and love each other very much.

IL: Ages 4-6

4.50 McPhail. **Andrew's Bath.** see Ch. 5.

4.51 Malloy. **Bad Thad.** see Ch. 3.

4.52 Newfield. **Where Did You Put Your Sleep?** see Ch. 3.

4.53 Nilsson, Ulf. **Little Sister Rabbit.** Boston: Atlantic Monthly Press, 1983. 30 pp.

Big brother rabbit is in charge of watching his sister while their parents gather carrots. He changes her diaper, reads a book, takes her for a walk, etc. After fixing her cereal, big brother puts his baby sister in her crib and goes to bed, exhausted by his day of babysitting.

IL: Ages 4-6

4.54 Ormerod. **Dad's Back.** see Ch. 8.

4.55 Ormerod, Jan. **101 Things to do with a Baby.** New York: Lothrop, Lee, and Shepard, 1984. 28 pp.

A resourceful older sister describes life in her house with a baby. Various ways the older sister amuses the baby such as fetching toys, playing peek-a-boo, and going for a walk are depicted. Big sister participates in the daily routines of bathing, dressing, and feeding her baby brother as well.

IL: Ages 4-6

4.56 Paterson, Diane. **Hey, Cowboy!** New York: Alfred A. Knopf, 1983. 42 pp.

When a little boy climbs on his grandfather's back for a horse ride, his older sister clamors for a turn. The little boy claims his sister must first provide a drink, then food, for the horse before she can ride. A sibling quarrel soon erupts which grandfather is able to divert by claiming it is his turn to ride.

IL: Ages 4-6

4.57 Pearson, Susan. **Saturday I Ran Away.** New York: J.B. Lippincott, 1981. 39 pp.

Katie decides to run away after several family incidents—she is wrongfully blamed for breaking something, her father rushes her out of the bathroom, and her older brother goes to play with friends and leaves Katie behind. As Katie prepares to leave, her brother and sister and both parents claim they envy her and would sometimes like to run away too. Katie then comes up with a plan where the entire family gets away from home for the day and all of them spend time doing activities they like the most.

IL: Ages 4-6

4.58 Pomerantz. **Posy.** see Ch. 8.

4.59 Rockwell, Anne and Harlow. **Can I Help?** New York: Macmillan, 1982. 22 pp.

A little girl demonstrates ways in which she helps her parents; she sets the table, rakes leaves, washes the car, etc. She realizes that there are certain tasks, such as cutting up vegetables, that she must be much older to do. Because she is so helpful, the little girl's mother and father are glad to assist her when she needs help as well.

IL: Ages 4-6

4.60 Rogers, Fred. **The New Baby.** New York: G.P. Putnam's Sons, 1985. 26 pp.

The emotions a child feels after the arrival of a new baby in the family are discussed—jealousy about the attention and gifts the baby receives, sadness because parents have less free time now, and even anger at always being told to "wait," "be quiet," and "be careful." However, the older brother or sister can talk about feelings and take pride in accomplishments and privileges that come with being older. It is stressed that the older child can eventually teach the baby new things and even help with its care. Most importantly, the older child and the baby are part of a family who care about one another, with plenty of love to go around.

IL: Ages 2-6

4.61 Rubel, Nicole. **Sam and Violet Are Twins.** New York: Avon Camelot, 1981. 30 pp.

Although Sam and Violet look alike, they are different in many other ways. When a teacher at school and the twin's aunt and uncle unfairly compare the twins, Sam and Violet rebel. Their parents decide to solve the problem by letting the twins select their own clothing to purchase and by focusing on the twins' individual likes and dislikes.

IL: Ages 4-6

4.62 Samuels, Barbara. **Faye and Dolores.** New York: Bradbury Press, 1985. 34 pp.

Older sister Faye becomes chagrined when young Dolores mimics her activities. Faye also likes to boss Dolores and remind her of foolish things she did as a baby. However, when the two sisters go to bed at night, Faye reassures Dolores about her fear of the dark.

IL: Ages 4-6

4.63 Sarnoff. **That's Not Fair.** see Ch. 3.

4.64 Sharmat. **Come Home, Wilma.** see Ch. 5.

4.65 Sharmat, Marjorie. **My Mother Never Listens to Me.** Niles, IL: Albert Whitman and Company, 1984. 26 pp.

In an effort to get his mother's attention, a little boy makes up exaggerated and shocking tales. His busy mother only responds with a monosyllabic answer. Only when the little boy requests a kiss, does his mother gladly stop what she's doing to respond.

IL: Ages 4-6

4.66 Sharmat, Marjorie. **Sometimes Mama and Papa Fight.** New York: Harper and Row, 1980. 31 pp.

Upset by their parents' quarreling, a brother and sister play pretend games and try singing so they won't have to listen. The boy wishes he could stop their quarrel or that he was sick so his parents would pay attention to him. As he is remembering another quarrel that was peacefully resolved, the boy notices it is quiet and his parents come upstairs to hug their children.

IL: Ages 4-6

4.67 Smith, Peter. **Jenny's Baby Brother.** New York: The Viking Press, 1981. 23 pp.

As her baby brother spends all his time sleeping, eating messily, and getting attention from her parents, Jenny feels he isn't much fun. However, when her brother starts throwing food at her, following her around, and causing her to stumble, Jenny's interest in him increases. Soon Jenny finds there are many things she can teach her brother and that playing with him can be quite amusing.

IL: Ages 4-6

4.68 Snell, Nigel. **Clare's New Baby Brother.** London: Hamish Hamilton, 1982. 24 pp.

Although quite satisfied with her life with a mother, a father, and a pet guinea pig, Clare helps her parents prepare for the arrival of a new baby. When her mother leaves for the hospital, grandmother comes to stay with Clare and comforts the little girl, who misses her mother. Clare is a great help to her mother in caring for the baby once it's home, but quite honestly declares that her guinea pig is much more fun.

IL: Ages 4-6

4.69 Stecher and Kandell. **Daddy and Ben Together.** see Ch. 8.

4.70 Tannenbaum, D. Leb. **Baby Talk.** New York: Avon Camelot, 1981. 27 pp.

Although his parents are wildly happy about the arrival of their new baby, Norris is not as excited. He can't understand all the sounds his baby sister makes, yet he tries to communicate with her. Norris is thrilled when his baby sister's first understandable word is his own name.

IL: Ages 4-6

4.71 Tax. **Families.** see Ch. 9.

4.72 Tester. **Jealous.** see Ch. 2.

4.73 Van Leeuwen, Jean. **Amanda Pig and Her Big Brother Oliver.** New York: E.P. Dutton, 1982. 56 pp.

Amanda is frustrated and feels left out when her older brother Oliver is able to do physical activities and play games which are too difficult for her. Likewise, Oliver is annoyed when his little sister tries to copy everything he does and when she refuses to let him dictate how they will play. Mother and Father Pig, with humor and great understanding, are able to soothe relationships between the two siblings.

IL: Ages 4-6

4.74 Van Leeuwen, Jean. **More Tales of Amanda Pig.** New York: E.P. Dutton, 1985. 56 pp.

In a series of five stories, Amanda Pig and her brother Oliver are involved in such activities as pretending they are the parents of a family of messy demanding children, deciding to clean their soiled stuffed animals in the bathtub, and trying to get along with a bunch of noisy cousins who come to visit. Amanda is also shown giving her father one of her special possessions for his birthday, but is relieved when father lends the stuffed animal to her at bedtime. In a final story, Amanda describes all the things she will do once she grows up and leaves home, yet claims she will never be too big to hug her mother.

IL: Ages 4-6

4.75 Walter Mildred. **My Mama Needs Me.** New York: Lothrop, Lee,
and Shepard, 1983. 29 pp.

When Jason's new baby sister comes home from the hospital, he
doesn't play with his friends because he is sure his mother will need
lots of help. Yet Jason is disappointed when his mother just wants to
sleep and he feels lonely and bored. Finally the baby awakens and
Jason helps with feeding and bathing his new sister. After his mother
assures Jason that she needs him very much, he goes to find his
friends.

IL: Ages 4-6

4.76 Warren. **Fred's First Day.** see Ch. 7.

4.77 Watson, Wendy. **Jamie's Story.** New York: Philomel, 1981. 22 pp.

A toddler very simply describes the activities experienced during a
day with mother and father. Father and mother each cook a meal and
share responsibility for child care. The child is happy to help out
with chores as much as possible.

IL: Ages 2-4

4.78 Weiss, Nicki. **Chuckie.** New York: Greenwillow Books, 1982. 29
pp.

Jealous of the attention her baby brother Chuckie is receiving, Lucy
begins misbehaving at home and neglecting her chores. She pretends
the baby isn't there, pushes him over, pulls his hair, etc.--none of
which seems to bother Chuckie in the least. Only when Chuckie's first
word happens to be her name, does Lucy have a change of heart
concerning her brother.

IL: Ages 4-6

4.79 Wells, Rosemary. **A Lion for Lewis.** New York: E.P. Dutton,
1982. 28 pp.

When young Lewis plays make-believe with his older brother and
sister, he is always given the least desirable role--the baby, the
patient, etc. Lewis puts on a lion suit and chases his brother and
sister around, pretending that he has been swallowed. This gives
Lewis equal standing with his older siblings.

IL: Ages 4-6

4.80 Wells, Rosemary. **Max's Bath.** New York: E.P. Dutton, 1985. 10
pp.

Big sister Ruby tries to give Max a bath but the orange sherbet all
over him turns one tubful of water orange and the grape juice he
drinks makes the next tubful purple. Finally Ruby gets Max
successfully clean in the shower, only to discover he has gotten her
dirty as well.

IL: Ages 2-4

4.81 Wells, Rosemary. **Max's Bedtime.** New York: E.P. Dutton, 1985. 10 pp.

Max is unable to fall asleep without his red rubber elephant. Trying to be helpful, big sister Ruby offers Max all her stuffed animals. Max's bed gets so crowded, he falls out and promptly finds his elephant under the bed.

IL: Ages 2-4

5

Fear and Fantasy

Fear is one of the more important emotions young children must learn to deal with. All children have a number of "typical fears" that are characteristic of each stage of development. As children grow older, overt fear responses are curbed by social pressure and children learn to avoid those situations that stimulate fear responses. Fantasy is another way in which young children learn to deal with their fears. Small children can create an imaginary companion to help them face a frightening situation. However, fantasy is also a way for children to derive pleasure, such as the creation of a make-believe friend that fills gaps in a child's life when other children are not available for play. Adults obviously play an important role in helping children to deal with the fears of childhood and in encouraging the fantasy activities that are an important part of a child's overall development.

Fear

All young children must learn to deal with the emotion of fear. Fear typically has a very specific source, such as fear of a vacuum cleaner or of loud noises. However, the source of fear is not always so easily traced. Many children will develop a fear of a dark bedroom. This type of fear is often related more to fantasies and dreams than to any real events in the child's life. Sometimes fears stem directly from developmental conflicts which the child may currently be struggling with, such as dependency and autonomy conflicts. Jersild and Holmes conducted the most extensive research on fears related to children in the two- to six-year-old range(1). This classic research gives insight into the many fears that children have during the early years that are often difficult to trace to a specific source. Jersild and Holmes report that younger children have particular fear of such things as strange people, certain kinds of objects, and falling. In contrast, children in the five- to six-year-old range show an increase in fear of imaginary or abstract things, such as fantasized creatures, robbers, the dark, death, being alone, or being ridiculed by others.

Fear is a very powerful emotion that is common to any stage of human development. It is an emotion that we all try to minimize or avoid. However, fear is a normal feeling and is an intricate part of a child's developmental process. In children, fears can occur at anytime with no particular warning. For example, a child for apparently no reason will suddenly develop an aversion to the bathtub or the dark. The most efficient way of helping a child try to overcome such fears is to help the child understand the fear as best possible and encourage the child to confront the fear in a supportive fashion. Using force or ridicule may have a very negative impact and ignoring fears will not make them go away. Fears are a normal part of development and should be confronted and openly dealt with by both the child and adult.

There are a number of specific factors that appear to be related to variation in children's fears. These factors are associated with mental and physical development as well as with individual experiences which determine what children learn to fear and how they learn to express their fears. The factors associated with these variations are(2):

Intelligence. Precocious children have fears characteristic of those of an older age level. For example, most three-year-olds have fears that are situationally determined; the precocious three-year-old, however, will usually have generalized and imaginary fears. Both generalized and imaginary fears are indicative of older children.

Sex. At all ages girls show more fears than boys as a group. Obviously, it has traditionally been more socially acceptable for girls to fear certain things such as bugs and snakes. This difference between boys and girls is probably socially defined.

Socioeconomic. Children from the lower classes at all ages show more fears than children from middle and upper class backgrounds.

Personality. Insecure children tend to be more easily frightened than children who are emotionally secure. The extroverted child appears to have more fears than the introverted child.

Ordinal position. Children who are firstborn have more fears than later born children. This is probably related to parental overprotectiveness of firstborn children. The more younger children associate with older siblings, the more fears that are learned.

Social contacts. Being with others who are frightened increases fear in children. Obviously adults are not immune to this sociological phenomenon.

Physical condition. If children are tired, hungry, or in poor health, they will respond with greater fear than children not confronted with these kinds of problems. These children will also be frightened in many situations which do not normally cause fear.

Fear differs dramatically in various individuals; however, the factors listed above are general categories that fear has been found to be associated with. It is noted that fear in children is not simply a stimulus-response kind of relationship, but dependent on a number of interrelated factors. One obviously cannot predict fear in children through the presence or absence of certain factors in the child's social environment. Each child is different and will respond to conditions associated with fear in various degrees.

Age is a key factor for determining fear responses. In babies, a fear response is typically one of helplessness. Crying is the most usual fear response. As children grow older, they hide their faces or get away as far as possible from the feared person or object. Very small children typically will hide behind their mother or behind a piece of furniture and remain there until the fear subsides or until they feel it is safe to emerge.

As children grow older, fear responses are curbed by social pressure. The crying reaction becomes less frequent and more socially acceptable ways determined by the child's age become more frequent. Typical reactions to fear by children in the early stages of development are retreat and withdrawal, imaginary ills, and false complaints. As children reach the ages of five or six, many learn to hide or disguise their feelings if fear is present. The tension and anxiety that co-vary with fear in the five- or six-year-old child may be dealt with psychologically in very sophisticated ways, in particular through defense mechanisms(3). Defense mechanisms can be used effectively to reduce tensions associated with certain kinds of fears. For the most part these mechanisms are normal and a healthy response to fear. Typical defense mechanisms employed are as follows:

Withdrawal. This is a very common defense mechanism in young children. It is the most direct defense possible; if a situation seems too difficult, the child simply runs away.

Denial. This is the refusal to admit that a situation exists or that an event even occurred. Children may react to a potent situation, such as the death of a pet, by pretending that the pet is still living in the house, eating in the kitchen, and sleeping with them at night.

Projection. This defense mechanism involves distortion of reality. Children, like adults who use this defense mechanism, attribute their own undesirable thoughts or actions to something else. This can be a person or object such as a stuffed animal or even a pet. Projection is complicated in that children may not know what they are escaping from and may not be able to understand feelings that go with this escape from reality.

Regression. Regression is an extreme form of denial in which children completely erase a frightening event or circumstance from their consciousness. They may literally not know an event occurred.

In younger children, the defense mechanisms of withdrawal and denial are generally most common. Most five- and six-year-old children use several of the defense mechanisms mentioned above. Rarely does a child use a single defense mechanism as a way of coping with fear and anxiety. As children grow older and mature, other defense mechanisms not mentioned above are sometimes used such as reaction formation and rationalization. It is felt that some defense mechanisms are learned by observing the behavior of parents or siblings. Most apparently are learned through the child's own experience of what defense works best to reduce fear and anxiety. Defense mechanisms that children learn during the preschool years often stay with them throughout a lifetime.

Fantasy

Fantasy is an important aspect of a child's social and emotional development. There has been some misunderstanding about the place of fantasy in the lives of small children. Several decades ago imaginary companions were viewed by many child specialists and parents as a neurotic use of imagination(4). Most professionals in the field of child development today feel that imaginary companions help children work through their problems. In fact, a child's periodic excursions into fantasy help to strengthen the child's contact with the real world(5). In other words, it becomes easier to tolerate the frustrations of the real world and to deal with the demands of reality through occasional journeys into fantasy.

Fantasy for young children is one important means through which children combat a number of childhood fears. Children will use imaginary friends, a teddy bear, or even an imaginary monster as a companion during a storm or when the child is afraid of the dark. By using fantasy in this way, fears common to childhood can be dealt with. As children grow older their intellectual development begins to replace fantasy as the most effective way of dealing with fear. Thus all children during their development use fantasy as a means of coping with the world around them; this process contributes to the child's emotional and social development.

Make-believe play appears at around eighteen months of age, continues to develop between ages three and four, peaks between five and six years, and then declines. Greta Fein indicates that when children engage in pretend play they have transformed the physical environment into a symbol(6). In pretend play, children try out many different roles--they may be the mother, the father, the teacher, the next-door neighbor, and so forth. Sometimes their pretend play reflects an adult role; at other times it may make fun of it.

Some research has been conducted on fantasy in childhood. In particular, a number of studies have explored factors in children related to fantasy play(7). Middleclass children, more so than lowerclass children, are likely to engage in fantasy play. The research concludes that boys engage in more fantasy play than girls. Small boys are more likely than girls to pretend that they are animals, pretend that objects are other things, and to attribute human feelings and behavior to inanimate objects. Research suggests that the sex differences found in fantasy play may reflect situational circumstances; for example, open spaces and materials favoring large-muscle activities facilitate fantasy play for boys. This position is consistent with the finding that boys engage in more pretend assaults than girls, who play more passive and physically restrained games.

Fantasy play should be encouraged in young children. Paraphernalia should be made available to children such as old shoes, clothes, and cardboard boxes. Parents and adults in general can likewise stimulate fantasy play by exploring a seashore or forest with a child. The late Dr. Anna Freud concluded that daydreams of children and fantasy experiences are the equivalent to free association of adults in psychotherapy. Just as Dr. Anna Freud felt free association was an effective tool in helping adults deal with emotional problems, children can deal with conflict and problems that are a part of childhood through fantasy(8).

Fear and Fantasy in Early Childhood Literature

During the preschool years, children are beset with a variety of fears; they may be frightened by storms with the accompanying thunder and lightning, by dogs or wild animals, by the thought of being lost from parents, or by the dark and the monsters who lurk within it. There are children's books available depicting characters possessing all these fears and more which a preschool child can readily identify with. In particular, a fear of the dark is a popular topic for early-childhood books and solutions to cope with this fear are varied, ranging from the use of a nightlight or flashlight to nightly inspections of a character's room and closet. An important element found in all the books concerning children's fears is the reassurance and understanding on the part of parents or another adult, with no denial of the fear or ridicule present.

Most children enjoy fantasy as a change from the here and now, as a breathing space in the serious process of growing up(9). With the many developmental changes that occur during the preschool years, it is evident why children from the ages of two to six delight in stories that spark their imagination. What fun to hear stories where toys come to life, where animals talk and exhibit human emotions, or where friendly monsters follow story characters around. Certainly most preschool children can identify with characters in books who, fed up with a child's life, assume the role of an adult or trade places with a pet for a short time. Many children will enjoy the fantasies of characters who travel to the moon when they can't sleep or who blame their own mischief on an imaginary friend.

Responses to the literature. Books depicting the very real emotion of fear can be comforting to the child who is frightened by a similar situation. The adult guide who reads such a book to a child or group of children will certainly want to encourage discussion from all children who feel inclined to do so. When fantasy is the theme of a picture book, children will probably want to talk about some of the imaginary, often amusing happenings as well.

Early-childhood books dealing with children's fears and fantasies would seem to be an excellent vehicle for provoking a wider range of responses to the literature. After consideration of a child's age and abilities, the adult reading aloud a book on such topics may wish to engage the child in activities such as:
1. Having a child hold up either a fairy wand (fantasy) or a ruler (reality) to distinguish between the two in a story being read aloud.
2. Using puppets to dramatize a common childhood fear, such as going to bed in a dark room, and ways to cope with the fear.
3. Pantomining by the child of an adult at work, a rag doll on a shelf, or a tired puppy.
4. Drawing or painting by the child of the most horrible monster imaginable, complete with name and a list of its hobbies, etc.
5. Using blobs of paint with folded paper to form ink blots, with the child determining what the blot represents(10).

All preschool children experience the emotion of fear at some time during their development. Although parents and other adults may try to reassure a child that fears are common to all children, no doubt a child would feel better discovering that a character in a book shares those fears. Adults also play a major role in encouraging fantasy play in children; the reading of books dealing with a character's flights into fantasy may serve to enhance the imagination of a child even more. The fears and fantasies of preschool children are not such a visible aspect of development as socializing with peers or the expression of anger and joy. For this reason, hearing stories concerning fears and fantasies and responding to such stories can help in the child's exploration of this important area of development.

NOTES

1. A. Jersild and F. Holmes, Children's Fears Child Development Monographs, No. 20 (New York: Columbia University Press, 1935).
2. Elizabeth B. Hurlock, Child Development 6th ed. (New York: McGraw-Hill, 1978), p. 198.
3. Grace J. Craig, Human Development 2d ed. (Englewood Cliffs, New Jersey: Prentice-Hall, 1980), p. 254.
4. Selma H. Fraiberg, The Magic Years (New York: Charles Scribner's Sons, 1959), p. 23.
5. Fraiberg, p. 23.
6. Greta Fein, Child Development (Englewood Cliffs, New Jersey: Prentice-Hall, 1978).
7. William J. Meyer and Jerome B. Dusek, Child Psychology-A Developmental Perspective (Lexington, Massachusetts: D.C. Heath and Company, 1979), p. 480.
8. Anna Freud and Dorothy Burlingham, Infants Without Families: The Case For and Against Residential Nurseries (New York: International Universities Press, 1944).
9. Zena Sutherland, Dianne Monson, and May Hill Arbuthnot, Children and Books 6th ed. (Glenview, Illinois: Scott, Foresman, and Company, 1981), p. 246.
10. Laura Broad and Nancy Butterworth, The Playgroup Handbook (New York: St. Martin's Press, 1974); Mary Platts, Launch: A Handbook of Early Learning Techniques for the Preschool and Kindergarten Teacher (Stevensville, Michigan: Educational Service Inc., 1972); Myra Sadker and David Sadker, Now Upon a Time-A Contemporary View of Children's Literature (New York: Harper and Row, 1977); Guy Wagner, Laura Gilloley, Betts Ann Roth, and Joan Cesinger, Games and Activities for Early Childhood Education (New York: Teachers Publishing, 1967).

BOOKS

5.1 Adams, Edith. **The Scaredy Book.** New York: Random House, 1983. 30 pp.

Wondering about the bed he'll sleep in, the food he'll eat, etc., Worried Walrus questions his decision to spend the night with a friend. Everything seems to go all right until the two friends go to bed. Then Walrus worries about creatures coming through the open window, thinks he sees a snake and tiger in the dark, and hears scary noises outside the window. Once his friend assures Walrus that he is only looking at shadows made by clothing and the noise outside is only rain, Walrus relaxes with a nightlight on and finally goes to sleep.

IL: Ages 4-6

5.2 Armitage. **The Bossing of Josie.** see Ch. 2.

5.3 Asch. **Goodnight Horsey.** see Ch. 8.

5.4 Asch, Frank. **Milk and Cookies.** New York: Parents Magazine Press, 1982. 36 pp.

During an overnight visit to his grandparent's house, Baby Bear wakes up in the night and sees his grandfather feeding a dragon in the cellar. Baby Bear then has a scary dream about the dragon, whom he must feed as well. After awakening everyone in the house, Baby Bear goes to the cellar with his father to discover the dragon is really only a glowing wood stove.

IL: Ages 2-6

5.5 Barsuhn, Rochelle. **Feeling Afraid.** Chicago: Children's Press, 1982. 29 pp.

Common fears such as being afraid of the dark, of storms, and of animals are described. Being afraid to make a new friend, to recite in front of a class, or to learn a new skill such as swimming is also discussed with children shown overcoming some of their fears.

IL: Ages 4-6

5.6 Berenstain, Stan and Jan. **The Berenstain Bears in the Dark.** New York: Random House, 1982. 29 pp.

When Brother Bear reads part of a scary mystery book to Sister and makes spooky sounds once they are in bed, Sister is unable to sleep and calls for help from her parents. Although Papa and Mama Bear try to reassure Sister, a practically sleepless night follows with Sister and Brother turning the bedroom light off and on. Only after Papa Bear finds a nightlight and Brother Bear reads her the not-so-scary ending of his book, can Sister Bear easily fall asleep the next night.

IL: Ages 4-6

5.7 Bonsall, Crosby. **Who's Afraid of the Dark?** New York: Harper and Row, 1980. 32 pp.

A small boy, who claims his dog is afraid of the dark, asks a friend for advice. Suspecting that the little boy is projecting his own fears, the friend tells him to hold, hug, and hang on to his dog that night. Following her advice seems to solve the little boy's problem.

IL: Ages 2-6

5.8 Bottner. **Mean Maxine.** see Ch. 2.

5.9 Boyd, Selma and Pauline. **I Met a Polar Bear.** New York: Lothrop, Lee, and Shepard, 1983. 28 pp.

Determined to arrive at school on time, a young boy is delayed when he helps a polar bear return to the zoo. Subsequently, an earthworm in need of a garden, an ant searching for his ant colony, and a pony whose rope is tangled in a tree all need the boy's assistance. Even as he explains his tardiness to the teacher, the boy looks out the window for another imaginary friend needing help.

IL: Ages 4-6

5.10 Brewster, Patience. **Nobody.** New York: Houghton Mifflin, 1982. 30 pp.

Whenever things don't go right for Sarah, she claims that "Nobody" is responsible for her misdeeds. "Nobody" becomes Sarah's companion at home and school, ready to help Sarah out whenever she needs it. Sarah's mother asks her to draw a picture of "Nobody" and Sarah is thrilled when she receives a "Nobody" doll for her birthday.

IL: Ages 4-6

5.11 Chess, Victoria. **Poor Esme'.** New York: Holiday House, 1982. 28 pp.

Her parents are always going out and the neighborhood children are always busy or already involved with friends, leaving young Esme' very lonely. Deciding she must have someone special to spend time with, Esme' tries wishing on a rainbow, after blowing out her birthday candles, upon throwing a coin in a fountain, etc. Desperate for a playmate, Esme' wishes on the first star of the night and is surprised and not altogether pleased when a new sibling arrives at her house a few weeks later.

IL: Ages 4-6

5.12 Chevalier. **Spence Isn't Spence Anymore.** see Ch. 8.

5.13 Chevalier, Christa. **Spence and the Sleepytime Monster.** Niles, IL: Albert Whitman and Company, 1984. 29 pp.

Claiming there's a monster in his bedroom, Spence makes his mother promise to come with a big stick if he calls for help. She searches

Spence's room and wonders out loud if the monster is imaginary. Sure enough a monstrous shape approaches Spence's bed and he proceeds to capture it in his blanket. As his mother suspected, Spence only caught his own black cat who cast a monstrous shadow on the wall.

IL: Ages 2-6

5.14 Chorao, Kay. **Lemon Moon.** New York: Holiday House, 1983. 27 pp.

A child tries to convince his grandmother that the shapes in his patchwork quilt come to life when it's dark. Claiming it was only a dream, Grandmother is nonetheless interested in the child's tale about animals leaping through the air and a yellow moon balloon floating above his bed. Trying to fall asleep once again, the child's fantasy reoccurs; he grabs the string on the moon balloon and floats in to take his grandmother for a ride.

IL: Ages 4-6

5.15 Christelow, Eileen. **Henry and the Dragon.** New York: Clarion Books, 1984. 29 pp.

After listening to a bedtime story about a dragon, Henry Rabbit is convinced he sees a dragon shadow on his dark wall and hears dragon noises outside his bedroom. Claiming the dragon is only in his imagination, Henry's parents nevertheless search his room and the bushes outside. When Henry thinks he sees and hears a dragon again the following night, his father searches outside again only to get caught in a dragon trap Henry has devised. Finally Henry discovers his very own baseball cap is producing the scary shadow.

IL: Ages 4-6

5.16 Counsel. **But Martin.** see Ch. 3.

5.17 Crowe, Robert. **Tyler Toad and the Thunder.** New York: E.P. Dutton, 1980. 27 pp.

Tyler Toad jumps into his hole at the first sign of thunder, something he fears. Various animal friends try to reassure Tyler about the thunder, saying it is only a noisy parade in the clouds, a patrol group testing their cannons, etc. Tyler finally emerges from his hole. But when an extra loud clap of thunder is heard, Tyler once again jumps to safety, only to find all his friends in his hiding hole as well.

IL: Ages 4-6

5.18 Cunliffe, John. **Sara's giant and the upside down house.** London: Andre' Deutsch, 1980. 31 pp.

Young Sara's mother scolds her for leaving toys and clothing lying about and declares the house is upside-down from the mess. Once her mother leaves for the store, Sara calls upon her giant friend who indeed turns her house upside down. Although Sara enjoys watching an upside down TV, having the furniture on the ceiling, and entering the house by climbing a tree and going through a window, her parents have more problems coping with the situation. When Sara's giant turns the house the right way once again, Sara's mother is so pleased she forgets to scold Sara for being untidy.

IL: Ages 4-6

5.19 Daly, Niki. **Joseph's Other Red Sock**. New York: Atheneum, 1982. 29 pp.

While getting dressed, Joseph finds that he has one red sock missing. With the help of his cat and some stuffed animals, Joseph searches his room and pulls a monstrous looking mound of clothes out of his cupboard. Only after grabbing at the monster and chasing it back into the cupboard does the pile of clothing surrender Joseph's red sock.

IL: Ages 4-6

5.20 de Regniers, Beatrice. **Waiting for Mama**. New York: Houghton Mifflin, 1984. 29 pp.

Amy is bored waiting outside the store for her mother. Then she starts to fantasize about waiting there the rest of her life--she marries, has children, and even becomes a grandmother. Just as her fantasy ends, Amy's mother reappears and Amy decides it wasn't such a long wait after all.

IL: Ages 4-6

5.21 Dickinson. **My Brother's Silly**. see Ch. 4.

5.22 Dillon, Barbara. **The Beast in the Bed**. New York: William Morrow and Company, 1981. 24 pp.

A small green beast, invisible to adults, moves into Marcia's house for the summer. The two friends are always together shopping, playing, and taking trips to the beach, but the beast gets nervous when Marcia starts preparing for school to start. Certain that Marcia will become so involved with school that she will soon ignore him, the beast sadly packs and leaves her home. Fortunately, the little green beast finds a preschool child the very next day and prepares to move in and become the child's constant companion.

IL: Ages 4-6

5.23 Dinan, Carolyn. **The Lunch Box Monster**. Boston: Faber and Faber, 1983. 28 pp.

A little boy carries two lunch boxes to school, one of which contains a huge green monster. According to the boy, his monster is responsible for scaring a teacher away, protecting him from a bully, and frightening people at a museum. The monster is also supposedly the one who messes up his owner's room, but the boy finds he must take the blame and clean up.

IL: Ages 4-6

5.24 Dragonwagon, Crescent. **If You Call My Name.** New York: Harper and Row, 1981. 25 pp.

A young girl claims that she might follow if a fish, hawk, or lion call her name and she imagines herself living in the wild with one of these creatures. However, if someone special (possibly a friend) calls her name, the little girl says she will definitely go and share wonderful times with that person.

IL: Ages 4-6

5.25 Drescher, Joan. **Max and Rufus.** Boston: Houghton Mifflin, 1982. 32 pp.

Tired of both their daily routines, Max and his dog decide to change places for a while. Although Max's dog enjoys his new role riding the school bus and sleeping in a comfortable bed, Max is not so happy being a dog when he is fed table scraps and gets taken to the dog pound. In a few days, Max and his dog are ready to resume their former roles.

IL: Ages 4-6

5.26 Feder, Jane. **The Night-Light.** New York: The Dial Press, 1980. 26 pp.

Uncomfortable with her dark room at bedtime, Kate declares she needs a nightlight. Although her mother lets Kate select a nightlight at a store the next day, it looks too scary at night. Kate then tries her overhead light which shines in her eyes, her flashlight which rolls off the bed, and her lamp which creates spooky shadows. Finally Kate discovers the best nightlight right outside her bedroom window--the familiar street lights in her neighborhood and the moon and stars in the sky.

IL: Ages 4-6

5.27 Gackenbach, Dick. **Little Bug.** New York: Houghton Mifflin, 1981. 29 pp.

A little bug plays it safe by hiding in a dark gloomy hole rather than facing the posibility of being pecked by a bird, squashed by a shoe, or captured in a jar. A mysterious voice reminds the little bug of the pleasures and adventure he is missing out on. Finally the little bug ventures out. Although he is still surrounded by dangers, the little bug is willing to take chances so he can better enjoy life.

IL: Ages 2-6

5.28 Gackenbach, Dick. **Poppy the Panda.** New York: Houghton Mifflin, 1984. 28 pp.

When Katie's panda bear refuses to go to bed because he has nothing nice to wear, Katie searches her room to remedy the situation. The panda refuses to wear a doll dress, doesn't care for roller skates, is unhappy with being wrapped in bathroom tissue, etc. Katie's mother finally solves the problem by tying a pretty ribbon around the panda bear's neck so that Katie and her bear can go to sleep.

IL: Ages 2-6

5.29 Galbraith. **Katie Did!** see Ch. 4.

5.30 Galloway. **When You Were Little and I Was Big.** see Ch. 8.

5.31 Glass. **My Brother Tries to Make Me Laugh.** see Ch. 3.

5.32 Gay, Michel. **Take Me for a Ride.** New York: William Morrow and Company, 1983. 24 pp.

Teddy climbs out of his stroller and pretends he is taking a butterfly for a ride. The butterfly is soon joined by a frog, duck, cat, fox, and bear. All the animals in turn give Teddy a ride in the stroller. When Teddy falls out, however, his fantasy ends and Teddy's mother comforts him.

IL: Ages 2-4

5.33 Goodspeed, Peter. **A Rhinoceros Wakes Me Up in the Morning.** Scarsdale, NY: Bradbury Press, 1982. 29 pp.

A little boy imagines that his stuffed animals help him throughout the day—an elephant brushes his teeth, a dragon makes his toast, a camel takes him home from school, a raccoon shampoos his hair, etc. The boy's zoo of stuffed animals all accompany him to bed as well.

IL: Ages 2-6

5.34 Greenleaf, Ann. **No Room for Sarah.** New York: Dodd, Mead, and Company, 1983. 29 pp.

When Sarah's many stuffed animals crowd her out of bed, Sarah's father insists that some of them have to go. Sarah tries letting some of the stuffed animals sleep on the floor and eventually gives some of them away to friends, but the animals are so upset and make such a racket each night that Sarah has to sleep with her parents. After three sleepless nights, Sarah's father comes up with a solution—they all build Sarah a huge wall-to-wall bed with plenty of room for Sarah and her menagerie.

IL: Ages 4-6

5.35 Hamilton. **How Do You Do, Mr. Birdsteps?** see Ch. 2.

5.36 Hamilton, Morse. **Who's Afraid of the Dark?** New York: Avon Camelot, 1983. 30 pp.

Claiming she can't sleep because her doll is so frightened of the dark bedroom, Kate urges her father to tell them a story. Each time he begins a story, Kate's father is interrupted by the doll who tells of her fears of wastebaskets, curtains, and noises outside. Kate and her father reassure the doll about her fears and after a brief story from father, Kate falls asleep.

IL: Ages 4-6

5.37 Hawkins, Colin and Jacqui. **Snap! Snap!** New York: G.P. Putnam's Sons, 1984. 27 pp.

Sally is startled to see a hairy green monster emerge from under her bed, especially when it carries her off for its supper. They join a group of squabbling monsters who all want to eat Sally, but she scolds them and hits them with her teddy bear. After the monster crowd apologizes, Sally takes them all to a playground where they have great fun until Sally wakes up in her bed.

IL: Ages 2-6

5.38 Hines, Anna. **Bethany for Real.** New York: Greenwillow Books, 1985. 21 pp.

Bethany makes a new friend who seems to enjoy pretending as much as she does. After Bethany shares a cup of pretend lemonade, the boy gives her a pretend kitten from a box he's carrying. An older girl is mad because Bethany is using her name and claims their pretend play is stupid. However, Bethany and her new friend are able to lure the older girl into participating in their fantasy as well.

IL: Ages 4-6

5.39 Hoban, Russell. **They Came from Aargh!** New York: G.P. Putnam's Sons, 1981. 24 pp.

Aboard their spaceship made of chairs, three children dressed as space travellers decide to land on Plovsnat, also known as Earth. There a mummosaurus (their mother) proceeds to tear their spaceship apart, yet offers a meal complete with chocolate cake. After promising to visit the mummosaurus again, the space travellers assemble their spaceship and blast off for another adventure.

IL: Ages 4-6

5.40 Hoffman. **Sister Sweet Ella.** see Ch. 4.

5.41 Jackson, Ellen. **The Bear in the Bathtub.** Reading, MA: Addison-Wesley, 1981. 28 pp.

As he dislikes taking a bath, Andrew is not displeased to discover his bathtub occupied by a bear. His parents, a policeman, and a group of firemen are all unsuccessful in removing the bear from Andrew's tub. As the days go by with Andrew unable to bathe, his friends refuse to play with him. Finally Andrew comes up with a plan--he lets the bear splash in the water and play with Andrew's toy boats, so that the bear willingly leaves the tub.

IL: Ages 4-6

5.42 Jackson, Ellen. **The Grumpus Under the Rug.** Chicago: Follett Publishing Company, 1981. 31 pp.

When marshmallows are poked in the typewriter, peanut butter is spread on the mirror, and toothpaste squirted in the telephone, a little boy claims that the Grumpus under the rug is responsible. His mother doesn't believe him and the little boy is punished each time. However, when mother stops to look under the rug, she discovers there is a Grumpus that she proceeds to throw out of the house.

IL: Ages 4-6

5.43 Jonas, Ann. **The Quilt.** New York: Greenwillow Books, 1984. 32 pp.

Excited about her new patchwork quilt, a young black girl searches the cloth squares for memories of nursery curtains, clothes worn long ago, and the fabric her stuffed dog is made of. As her bedroom grows darker, the little girl imagines that her stuffed dog is lost and that the quilt becomes a town, a circus, a lake with boats, a tunnel, and finally a forest. Awakening the next morning, the little girl finds her dog at the edge of the quilt.

IL: Ages 4-6

5.44 Jones, Rebecca. **The Biggest, Meanest, Ugliest Dog in the Whole Wide World.** New York: Macmillan, 1982. 28 pp.

Frightened of the huge dog that lives next door, Jonathan runs into his house, crosses the street, or climbs a tree whenever he sees it. When the dog comes into Jonathan's yard and approaches him, Jonathan throws a ball at it. This becomes a game and is the beginning of a friendship between Jonathan and the dog.

IL: Ages 2-6

5.45 Jong. **Megan's Book of Divorce.** see Ch. 9.

5.46 Joosse. **The Thinking Place.** see Ch. 3.

5.47 Kent. **Knee-High Nina.** see Ch. 6.

5.48 Krensky, Stephen. **The Lion Upstairs.** New York: Atheneum, 1983. 40 pp.

None of his family is interested when Sam plays safari and captures an imaginary lion. When Sam uses his lion as an excuse for food disappearing and for chores not getting done, his parents and older sister makes plans to blame the lion for Sam's lack of allowance as well. Deciding his imaginary lion is causing too much trouble, Sam declares to his family that he sent it back to Africa, at least for a while.

IL: Ages 4-6

5.49 Levenson. **When I Grow Up and You Grow Down.** see Ch. 8.

5.50 Le-Tan, Pierre. **Visit to the North Pole.** New York: Crown Publishers, 1980. 25 pp.

Constant companions Alex and his stuffed polar bear hide beneath the covers each night and go on an adventure. During a bedtime visit to the North Pole, the two friends visit penguins, talk to a reindeer, go ice fishing, etc. Alex and his bear return home and reappear from beneath the covers just as mother comes in to say good night.

IL: Ages 4-6

5.51 Lobe, Mira. **Valerie and the Good-Night Swing.** New York: Oxford University Press, 1982. 30 pp.

Unwilling to go to bed, Valerie plays on her swing and dons a variety of hats which help her to fantasize. A towel turban takes her to the land of camels and bazaars, a rainhat places her aboard a ship, a red scarf turns Valerie into a farmer's wife, a conductor's cap helps her board a train, and a stocking cap takes Valerie to a snowy ski village. Finally Valerie grows tired and her father carries her from the fantasy swing to her bed, removing the last hat.

IL: Ages 4-6

5.52 Low, Joseph. **Don't Drag Your Feet...** New York: Atheneum, 1983. 38 pp.

Disgusted because her toys are unable to talk, Peggy does not treat them very nicely at times. During a dream, Peggy's wish that her toys could talk comes true. After dreaming that her toys converse with each other, ignoring Peggy and sometimes mistreating her, Peggy is happy to wake up and decides to show her toys more respect.

IL: Ages 4-6

5.53 McKee, David. **Not Now, Bernard.** New York: Methuen, 1980. 24 pp.

Bernard's parents tend to ignore him even when he claims that there is a monster in the garden. The monster eats Bernard and takes his place in the household. However, Bernard's parents are oblivious to Bernard's replacement as they give the monster Bernard's dinner, let it watch TV, and tuck the monster into bed.

IL: Ages 4-6

5.54 McPhail, David. **Andrew's Bath.** Boston: Little, Brown, and Company, 1984. 32 pp.

Tired of Andrew's complaints about their assisting him at bath time, Andrew's parents declare he is old enough to give himself a bath. While Andrew's parents call out instructions, Andrew claims that a menagerie of wild animals is preventing him from washing, shampooing, etc. Nevertheless, he is eventually clean and dressed in pajamas. Andrew then says goodnight to his very weary parents.

IL: Ages 4-6

5.55 McPhail, David. **The Dream Child.** New York: E.P. Dutton, 1985. 28 pp.

As the moon rises, the Dream Child and her teddybear awaken and sail through the sky in a winged boat. The Dream Child is able to soothe a restless lion, bring laughter to a group of angry giants, join the dance of an ape family, and free a needy giraffe. A visit to teddybear's mother is also included before the two weary travellers climb back aboard their boat.

IL: Ages 2-6

5.56 McPhail, David. **Pig Pig Rides.** New York: E.P. Dutton, 1982. 20 pp.

When Pig Pig's mother inquires about his plans for the day, Pig Pig responds excitedly. Not only does he plan to jump over 500 elephants on his motorcycle and drive a train to China, Pig Pig also claims he'll probably take a rocket to the moon. Pig Pig's mother only requests that he be careful and return before dark.

IL: Ages 2-4

5.57 Maris, Ron. **Are you there, Bear?** New York: Greenwillow Books, 1984. 29 pp.

When it is discovered that a teddybear is missing in a dark bedroom, toys come to life one by one and join in the search. The teddybear is finally found sitting in a chair with a book and the other toys request that he read them a story.

IL: Ages 2-6

5.58 Martin, Jacqueline. **Bizzy Bones and Uncle Ezra.** New York: Lothrop, Lee, and Shepard, 1984. 29 pp.

After moving into an old shoe with his uncle, Bizzy feels warm and comfortable throughout the winter until the March winds begin to blow. Bizzy then worries about the two of them and the shoe house blowing away. He stuffs rocks into both their pockets and Bizzy's uncle ties their shoe to a tree and a rock wall in an effort to calm his nephew's fears. Only when his uncle makes a carousel which uses the wind for power does Bizzy relax and enjoy his new toy.

IL: Ages 4-6

5.59 Murphy, Jill. **What Next, Baby Bear!** New York: E.P. Dutton, 1983. 29 pp.

Although his mother claims he can not go to the moon, Baby Bear searches his home for a rocket, space helmet, and other items he needs for his journey. With everything packed in his rocket made of a cardboard box, Baby Bear goes up the chimney through the clouds and lands on the moon. Finding the moon boring, Baby Bear has a picnic and proceeds to return home, just as his mother calls him to take a bath for bedtime.

IL: Ages 2-4

5.60 Oram. **Angry Arthur.** see Ch. 2.

5.61 Parenteau, Shirley. **I'll Bet You Thought I Was Lost.** New York: Lothrop, Lee, and Shepard, 1981. 27 pp.

During a grocery shopping excursion with his father, Sandy becomes lost. Although he anxiously searches each aisle of the store and sees many shopping carts which look familiar, Sandy is unable to locate his father. Finally resolving to live at the store until his family's next shopping trip, Sandy runs into his father and pretends he wasn't afraid at all.

IL: Ages 4-6

5.62 Park, Ruth. **When the Wind Changed.** New York: Coward, McCann, and Geoghegan, 1980. 28 pp.

Josh is very good at making faces and is able to scare dogs, his grandmother, etc. Josh's father warns him that if the wind changes while he is making a face, Josh's face will stay that way. When this indeed happens, Josh is able to thwart a bank robbery with his scary face and becomes a hero.

IL: Ages 4-6

5.63 Robison, Deborah. **No Elephants Allowed.** New York: Houghton Mifflin, 1981. 28 pp.

Justin worries about the elephants who enter his bedroom each night, especially when they are joined by lions and alligators. Although they claim that wild animals couldn't possibly be in his room, his father gives him a stuffed rabbit, his mother builds him a new bed, and Justin's sister provides him with a nightlight all in an effort to help. Nothing seems to work until Justin comes up with his own solution—he hangs up a scary gorilla picture on the wall to protect him from the wild animals.

IL: Ages 4-6

5.64 Ross. **Naughty Nicky.** see Ch. 3.

5.65 Ryder, Joanne. **The Night Flight.** New York: Macmillan, 1985. 31 pp.

After an evening playing in the park, Anna runs home as she notices darkness approaching. Once she is tucked into bed, Anna listens to the night sounds and dreams of flying through the window into the night outside. Anna soars over the city to the park, where goldfish whisper to her, a lion takes her for a ride on his back, and the park is transformed into a jungle with a waterfall. Upon awakening, Anna tells her mother about her flying adventure and hurries off to the park.

IL: Ages 4-6

5.66 Ryder, Joanne. **The Snail's Spell.** New York: Frederick Warne, 1982. 28 pp.

A child imagines shrinking in size, becoming soft and grey, having no appendages, and being unable to walk or run. As the child continues to fantasize about gliding along the ground making use of feelers and curling into a shell, it is evident that the child is pretending to be a snail.

IL: Ages 4-6

5.67 Schubert, Ingrid and Dieter. **There's a Crocodile Under My Bed!** New York: McGraw Hill, 1981. 23 pp.

Although her father can not find it in her room, Peggy claims she can't sleep because of the alligator under her bed. The alligator, who happens to be friendly, delights Peggy with an evening of playing in the bathtub, dancing, and making an alligator model out of boxes. As Peggy grows sleepy, her alligator friend tells her the story of his need to be nice to human children as penance for his past life of scaring young animals. Although her parents discover the cardboard alligator the next day and think it explains Peggy's story, she knows better.

IL: Ages 4-6

5.68 Schwartz. **Bea and Mr. Jones.** see Ch. 8.

5.69 Sharmat, Mitchell. **Come Home, Wilma.** Chicago: Albert Whitman and Company, 1980. 29 pp.

Sent to her room for hitting her brother, Wilma angrily fantasizes about running away. In her fantasy, she does all the things her mother disapproves of and performs dangerous feats until her mother begs for her to stop and come home. Wilma apologizes to her mother and the two make up by hugging and planning an outing together.

IL: Ages 4-6

5.70 Sharmat, Marjorie. **Frizzy the Fearful.** New York: Holiday House, 1983. 29 pp.

Frizzy Tiger is scared of practically everything and constantly makes up excuses to keep his friends unaware of his fears. Although he is terrified of leaving his house, Frizzy must venture out for groceries. He encounters a mud puddle, swinging doors, and a juicy lemon--all things that he fears, causing him to run home. When Frizzy sees a friend in trouble, however, he must conquer his fear of climbing to rescue her and decides to face the mud puddle next.

IL: Ages 4-6

5.71 Sharmat. **My Mother Never Listens to Me.** see Ch. 4.

5.72 Shecter, Ben. **The Discontented Mother.** New York: Harcourt Brace Jovanovich, 1980. 29 pp.

After Orin spends a day misbehaving, his mother pleads with him to change. Orin then proceeds to turn himself into a variety of animals, none of which pleases his mother. When Orin becomes a walrus, his mother is finally satisfied and she decides to be a mother walrus.

IL: Ages 4-6

5.73 Small, David. **Imogene's Antlers.** New York: Crown Publishers, 1985. 26 pp.

When Imogene awakes one morning to find she has grown antlers, she finds dressing and going through doors difficult, but the rest of her day is fine. The school principal is called in for advice, a doctor comes to examine Imogene, and her mother faints repeatedly. Imogene's resourceful brother uses her antlers for a candelabra and has a huge hat made to cover the antlers. The next morning Imogene's family is overjoyed to see the antlers have disappeared, until they notice Imogene has grown a peacock's tail.

IL: Ages 4-6

5.74 Smith, Susan. **The Night Light.** Chicago: Follett Publishing Company, 1981. 31 pp.

Although William the bug is not frightened by such things as spiders, the wind, or deep water, he is afraid of the dark. William temporarily solves his problem by capturing a lightning bug to use in his bedroom. The lightning bug wants his freedom so he teaches William how to always have a night light--by closing his eyes and thinking about light, bright things.

IL: Ages 2-6

5.75 Snell, Nigel. **Danny is Afraid of the Dark.** London: Hamish Hamilton, 1982. 26 pp.

Danny hurriedly prepares for bed, certain that there are monsters lurking in the dark corners of his bedroom. When Danny calls for help, his mother comes and reassures Danny that he only imagined the monsters. Two monsters then leave Danny's room, sad that he doesn't believe in them anymore.

IL: Ages 4-6

5.76 Stevenson, James. **We Can't Sleep.** New York: Greenwillow Books, 1982. 30 pp.

Claiming they are unable to sleep for various reasons, Louie and Mary Ann are eager to hear a story from their grandfather. Grandpa describes a sleepless night he had as a child and what he did to get tired, such as swimming across the ocean, running 50 miles, and fighting a dragon. At the completion of Grandpa's story which concludes with him safe at home, Mary Ann and Louie have fallen asleep.

IL: Ages 4-6

5.77 Stevenson, James. **What's Under My Bed?** New York: Greenwillow Books, 1983. 30 pp.

When his two grandchildren are too scared to fall asleep, Grandpa tells them a story about being afraid at bedtime as a child. As he describes his sleepless night with all the scary shapes he saw and frightening sounds he heard, the grandchildren come up with logical explanations for each happening. Claiming that he was finally able to sleep that night after eating a snack, the grandchildren decide to try his solution as well.

IL: Ages 4-6

5.78 Stoddard, Sandol. **Bedtime Mouse.** Boston: Houghton Mifflin, 1981. 32 pp.

Reluctant to go to bed, a child imagines that the toys in his room are enlarged and able to participate in all types of adventures. The toys eventually create bedlam in the child's room. A stuffed elf urges the child to keep the toys quiet and go to bed, where the child will be able to fantasize about secrets and surprises in his dreams.

IL: Ages 2-4

5.79 Stren, Patti. **I'm Only Afraid of the Dark (at Night!!)** New York: Harper and Row, 1982. 38 pp.

Harold the owl, who lives with his family at the Arctic Circle, doesn't like the dark and hates to close his eyes. Since winter is approaching with 24 hours a day of darkness, a friend who shares Harold's fear decides to help him overcome it. The two friends work together until Harold is able to face the darkness without a flashlight.

IL: Ages 4-6

5.80 Sussman, Susan. **Hippo Thunder.** Niles, IL: Albert Whitman and Company, 1982. 28 pp.

The members of a child's family each have an explanation for the loud sound that thunder makes--sister says the angels are bowling, brother explains that the stars are snoring, and grandma claims the flowers are being awakened. However, the child is not reassured about his fear and heads for his parents' room. Father teaches the child how to count between the lightning and thunder to gauge how far away the storm is and stays with the child until the storm passes.

IL: Ages 4-6

5.81 Szilagyi, Mary. **THUNDERSTORM.** Scarsdale, NY: Bradbury Press, 1985. 29 pp.

While busily playing in her sandbox, a little girl looks up to see a thunderstorm approaching and she and her dog run toward the house. The little girl's mother, who knows about her fear of storms, comforts the crying child and the two watch the thunderstorm together. The little girl in turn comforts her trembling dog and once the storm passes, she and the dog go back to the sandbox.

IL: Ages 2-6

5.82 Tallon, Robert. **The Alligator's Song.** New York: Parent's Magazine Press, 1981. 38 pp.

Certain that he sees an alligator outside his window, Eddie tells his mother but is sent back to bed. Eddie sees the alligator again and decides to help the sad alligator find its way home. The very next night, Eddie is once again sent back to bed when he discovers a white elephant wanting to return to its jungle.

IL: Ages 4-6

5.83 van der Meer, Ron and Atie. **I'm fed up!** London: Hamish Hamilton, 1981. 28 pp.

Tired of being bossed around, four year old Paula acquires the ability to turn herself into someone or something else. Although being a dog, tree, angel, and circus performer all seem desirable at first, Paula finds that each role has its drawbacks. Becoming Cinderella most certainly convinces Paula to be herself again.

IL: Ages 4-6

5.84 Ward. **Giant.** see Ch. 3.

5.85 Watts. **Zebra Goes to School.** see Ch. 7.

5.86 Watanabe, Shigeo. **I'm the king of the castle.** New York: G.P. Putnam's Sons, 1981. 28 pp.

A young bear discovers it is fun to play all by himself. Through the use of his imagination, the bear is able to create exciting adventures. His ability to play independently makes the bear feel proud.

IL: Ages 2-4

5.87 Weiss, Nicki. **Waiting.** New York: Greenwillow Books, 1981. 27 pp.

A little girl, who finds it difficult to await her mother's return home, imagines that she hears, smells, and even feels her mother. The child is so lost in thought that her mother's return surprises her.

IL: Ages 2-4

5.88 Wells. **A Lion for Lewis.** see Ch. 4.

5.89 Wells, Rosemary. **Good Night, Fred.** New York: The Dial Press, 1981. 28 pp.

Fred is very upset when his bouncing on the couch breaks the telephone because he thinks his grandmother is inside it. Fred's older brother sends Fred off to bed as he frantically tries to repair the phone. Coming downstairs later, Fred urges his grandmother to come out of the phone and the two of them have a wonderful time until Fred's brother arrives to tuck him into bed.

IL: Ages 4-6

5.90 Willis, Jeanne. **The Tale of Fearsome Fritz.** New York: Holt, Rinehart, and Winston, 1982. 24 pp.

Fearsome Fritz delights in activities such as dressing up or jumping out of closets to scare others, especially his parents. When Fritz wears a gorilla suit to the zoo, he has fun frightening the people there. However, when Fritz is mistaken for a real gorilla and locked up in a cage, he is not so happy.

IL: Ages 4-6

6

Motor Development and Physical Change

Separating motor and physical development from cognitive development in preschool children is a difficult task. Preschool children understand the world in terms of information they receive from their own bodies, perceptions, motor activity, and the ways in which they experience themselves. Virtually everything a child does from birth through the first few years lays the base, in some way, for not only later motor and physical development, but for cognitive, social, and emotional development as well(1). Much of what preschool children do is sheer sensory exploration--making mud pies, crawling, or climbing. The preschool child explores places and objects to find out what they feel like, to hear them, and to see them.

Many aspects of development proceed from a motor and physical base. Some developmental sources are continuous, as in the natural progression from scribbling to writing, while others are not. For example, children may explore different weaves and textures of material randomly at first with their fingers and eyes before they are ready to sort and classify, or compare and contrast. In a very similar way they must sort and compare thoughts before they can deal with complex ideas. Motor and physical development is a useful starting point from which to understand other kinds of more complex developmental activities related to cognitive and emotional development.

Physical Development

The early-childhood years are a time of much physical growth and change. The average boy and girl grows about two-and-one-half inches and gains between five and seven pounds a year during early childhood. During the preschool years, both boys and girls slim down as the trunk of their bodies becomes longer. Although their heads are still somewhat large for their bodies, by the end of the preschool years most children have lost the look that makes them seem top-heavy(2). Body fat slowly declines and the chubby baby will look much leaner by the end of the early-childhood years. As might be expected, girls have more fatty tissue than boys.

Clearly, there is much variation in growth patterns of children. The variation in height is mainly due to genetic factors; obviously environment plays a role as well. For example, in reviewing more than 200 studies of the heights of preschool children around the world, it was concluded that the two most important contributers to height differences are ethnic origin and nutrition. Urban, middle-class, firstborn children were taller than rural, lower-class, and later born children, possibly because the former experience better health care and nutrition. In the United States, height differences among preschool children are mainly due to genetic inheritance because most children receive enough food for their bodies to grow appropriately(3).

Motor Skills

A number of important motor skills develop during the preschool years. Several studies have been conducted on motor skills learned during the years from two to six. The skills that children are expected to learn are mainly those involving the hands and arms and those involving the legs and feet. Because maturation of muscle coordination follows the laws of developmental direction, hand skills can be learned earlier than leg skills. Hand skills, for the most part, are more useful to children than leg skills, so they are better learned and of better quality than leg skills for the preschool child(4).

Hand skills. Control of the muscles of the arms, shoulders, and wrists improves dramatically during the preschool years. Control of the fine muscles in the fingers, however, develops at a slower rate. Children cannot write at a speedy rate or play musical instruments well until around the age of twelve or older(5).

Self feeding is one important hand skill mastered during infancy and the preschool years. A baby typically cannot hold a bottle placed in the mouth until around eight months. By the time children are eleven or twelve months old, they can hold a cup temporarily and try to feed themselves with a spoon. By the end of the second year, young children can use forks as well as spoons. During the third year, they can spread jam or butter on their bread with a knife. Roughly a year later, most children, if given the opportunity, can cut tender meat with a knife. By the time the child is six, all the tasks used in self feeding have usually been mastered.

Ball throwing and catching are other hand skills that develop during the early-childhood years. Some babies roll and may even attempt to throw balls before they are two years old. However, even at age four, most preschool children cannot throw a ball well. By six years of age, most children are proficient though there are marked variations at every age(6).

Catching a ball is a far more difficult motor skill. At age four, few children can catch a ball, while at age six roughly two-thirds are able to. Initially, children use the whole body to grasp the ball when it is thrown to them. Then they use arms, with random movement. Six-years-olds begin to perfect a coordinated movement of the hands to catch the ball between the palms.

Dressing skills are also an important accomplishment during the preschool years. Two- and three-year-olds can often undress before they are able to put clothing on. By the age of five, children can generally manage buttons and zippers and may even be able to tie shoelaces.

Leg skills. If one looks closely at the development of leg skills of children in the first few years of life, the changes are quite dramatic. Before age two, babies can typically walk sideways and backwards; they can stand on one foot with help, and a year later, without help. Children can also usually walk on tiptoe by this time. The two-year-old, who is still rather short and a bit rounded, will walk with a wide stance and a body sway. However, overall physical development at this age is much more advanced than the infant's. By the time the child is three, the child's legs are closer together during walking and running, and the child does not have to constantly check what the feet are doing(7).

Climbing occurs even before walking. A baby first learns to climb stairs by creeping and crawling. Before children are two years old, they can walk upstairs and downstairs with help, that is, by holding the hand of an older person or a railing. Gradually, with practice, children let go of the older person or stair rail and are able to climb steps similar to the way an adult does.

By the time the child is four, physical development allows the child to vary the rhythm of running; four-year-olds are even able to skip. Between the ages of five and six, physical development usually allows the child to walk on a balance beam confidently, to follow a chalk mark on the floor, and even to imitate dance steps(8).

Tricycling and bicycling are skills that typically cannot be mastered until around three to four years of age. After a child develops the ability to ride a tricycle, much self-confidence follows. The child can eventually ride forward or backward and even ride while standing up. Children usually move from the tricycle to a bicycle by the age of six. Riding a bicycle is a very difficult and complex skill. A child may need six months to a year of practice before riding without falls or other accidents.

Learning Physical-Motor Skills

The physical-motor skills that preschool children learn are usually everyday actions, such as cutting and crayon skills, feeding themselves, dressing skills, and skipping and jumping. Developmental specialists in other parts of the world put great emphasis on the value of early training in motor skills such as gymnastics and music. American psychologists, on the other hand, after some unsuccessful attempts during the 1930s to train children in physical-motor skills, have come to believe that young children learn best with a minimum of training and a maximum of free exploration(9). Despite this difference in opinion about whether or not to train a young child, it is helpful to look at the following factors related to physical-motor learning.

Readiness. Any new skill or learning experience generally requires a state of readiness on the part of the child. A certain degree of maturation, some prior learning, and a number of preliminary skills must be present before the child can profit from training. It is difficult, however, to know when children have reached the point of readiness. At this point, children want to learn, enjoy the practice, and get excited over their own performance. Children themselves are often the best indicators of when they have reached the point of optimal readiness--they begin to imitate particular skills on their own(10).

Motivation. Children usually try out new things just to see if they can do them, to test their muscles, and to enjoy the way it feels. They run, jump, climb, and skip just for the pleasure it brings them. This kind of motivation, which comes from within the child, is intrinsic. Extrinsic motivation, in the form of parental encouragement, peer competition, etc., can also prompt a child to attempt a certain skill.

Activity. Activity is essential to motor development. When children are raised in limited and restricted environments, the development of their physical-motor skills lags. On the other hand, children who have a rich, meaningful environment full of objects, open space, and people to imitate have great opportunities to practice and perfect skills. Self-designed and self-paced schedules of learning are often more efficient than some adult-programmed "lessons"(11).

Feedback. Learning motor skills is definitely motivated by feedback. Intrinsic feedback is an important trigger for skill development. The young child may like the feeling of tension in the muscles or the experience of being up high. Extrinsic feedback comes in the form of rewards, such as candy or praise for a task well done.

If children are not encouraged to try out new motor skills that they are capable of doing, these skills will be slow to develop. Environmental stimulation--in the form of recognizing readiness, motivating through encouragement, insuring there are opportunities for activity, or providing feedback--plays an important role in a child's physical-motor development.

Motor Development and Physical Change in Early Childhood Literature

Physical development proceeds very rapidly during the preschool years. This development is quite accurately reflected in literature for children of this age group. Where the two-year-old character in a book may be depicted with a stocky solid build, the five- and six-year-old often has a much sleeker body in book illustrations. Preschool children are understandably curious about physical changes in their bodies. Therefore, books which compare the preschooler's physical development to that of an infant are valuable. To even better illustrate the progression of growth, literature which very simply discusses prenatal development can satisfy the questions posed by a preschooler, especially the child who is expecting a new baby in the household.

As children mature physically, they gain more control over the body. How the preschooler loves movement--running, riding a trike, swinging, rocking on a rocking horse, or sliding down a slanted incline(12). Children's literature depicts this love of motor activity.

Characters who are proud of learning to feed or dress themselves can be found in picture books, as well as those who are mastering the riding of a bike or climbing to the top of a jungle gym. Encouragement given by parents as a motivator for the character is a common theme, as is the character's wish to keep up with peers.

Responses to the literature. Certainly most preschoolers can identify with characters in books who proudly display their new motor skills. Hearing about such a character may be the impetus for a preschool child to keep trying to master those difficult tasks of handling buttons or zippers, or throwing and catching a ball. The adult guide must remember that children acquire motor skills at different chronological ages and that children increase in height and weight at varying rates as well. Therefore, after reading a book on these topics, discussions involving preschool children in a group should be sensitive to these individual differences. The adult guide may wish to encourage additional responses to the literature by:

1) Having children try on some of their own outgrown clothing to see how much they have changed in size.

2) Tracing a full size outline of a child on paper, with the child adding facial features, clothing, and so on.

3) Pantomining by the child of dressing or feeding skills, with other children or an adult trying to identify them.

4) Making outlines of an adult hand with a baby's hand inside it, then tracing the preschool child's hand between the two for comparison.

5) Having children draw or paint a picture of something that they can do now that couldn't be done at age two, three, etc.(13)

As children grow and develop, they find out what their bodies can do. In addition to the personal thrill a preschooler often feels at learning a new motor skill, the child needs motivation from supportive adults as well. An awareness of bodily changes and motor accomplishments has a positive effect on preschool children's self-images and promotes their understanding of other areas of development.

NOTES

1. Grace J. Craig, **Human Development** 2d ed. (Englewood Cliffs, New Jersey: Prentice-Hall, 1980), p. 226.

2. John W. Santrock and Steven R. Yussen, **Children and Adolescents-A Developmental Perspective** (Dubuque, Iowa: William C. Brown, 1984), p. 168.

3. Santrock and Yussen, p. 168.

4. Elizabeth B. Hurlock, **Child Development** 6th ed. (New York: McGraw-Hill, 1978), p. 508.

5. Hurlock, p. 146.

6. Hurlock, p. 146.

7. Craig, p. 227.

8. Hurlock, p. 147.

9. Craig, p. 228.

10. Craig, p. 230.

11. Craig, p. 230.

12. Margaret C. Gillespie and John W. Conner, **Creative Growth through Literature for Children and Adolescents** (Columbus, Ohio: Charles E. Merrill, 1975), p. 71.

13. Viola S. Carmichael, **Curriculum Ideas for Young Children** (Los Angeles: Southern California Association for the Education of Young Children, 1974); Doreen Croft and Robert Hess, **An Activities Handbook for Teachers of Young Children** (Boston: Houghton Mifflin, 1975); Don Dinkmeyer, **Developing Understanding of Self and Others (DUSO) Manual** (Circle Pines, Minnesota: American Guidance Service, 1970).

BOOKS

6.1 Andersen. **What's the Matter, Sylvie, Can't You Ride?** see Ch. 8.

6.2 Barbato. **From Bed to Bus.** see Ch. 8.

6.3 Barrett, Judi. I'm **too small.** YOU'RE TOO BIG. New York: Atheneum, 1981. 31 pp.

A young boy compares his physical size and capabilities to those of his father. Although the boy feels there are drawbacks to being small, he realizes that there are advantages as well. He also knows that someday he'll be as big as his father, maybe even bigger.

IL: Ages 2-4

6.4 Brooks, Robert. **So That's How I Was Born!** New York: Little Simon, 1983. 36 pp.

After he hears about how babies are born from a playmate, Joey questions his parents about this information. Joey's parents quite simply answer each of his questions concerning fertilization of the egg, the growth of a baby during pregnancy, and the actual birth process. Differences in the male and female body are also discussed in a relaxed manner and Joey is aware that his parents will answer other questions he has concerning sex in the future.

IL: Ages 4-6

6.5 Brown. **Someone Special, Just Like You.** see Ch. 10.

6.6 Bruna, Dick. **When I'm big.** New York: Methuen, 1981. 24 pp.

A young child thinks about all the physical skills that can be accomplished in the future--swimming, dancing, skating, playing tennis, etc. Other accomplishments such as playing a musical instrument, drawing, and collecting stamps are considered as well.

IL: Ages 4-6

6.7 Cohen. **No Good in Art.** see Ch. 8.

6.8 Cohen. **So What?** see Ch. 8.

6.9 Cole, Joanna. **How You Were Born.** New York: William Morrow and Company, 1984. 48 pp.

With the use of photographs, the development of a baby within the mother's womb is quite simply explained. Fertilization of the egg cell and the birth of a baby are also described. The first few accomplishments of an infant are stated as the beginning of learning many new things as a part of growing up.

IL: Ages 4-6

6.10 Elliot, Dan. **Two Wheels for Grover.** New York: Random House, 1984. 32 pp.

During Grover's visit to his cousins who live in the country, he feels embarrassed because he is unable to ride a bike. When his cousins go on bike rides, Grover comes up with an excuse each day--his mother won't let him, he has a sore foot, or he ate too much. Suspecting that Grover hasn't learned to ride a bike yet, Grover's older cousin patiently gives him lessons which soon pay off.

IL: Ages 4-6

6.11 Fitzhugh, Louise. **I Am Four.** New York: Delacorte Press, 1982. 43 pp.

A four-year old girl describes her many accomplishments: she likes to draw, helps set the table, ties her shoes, and is a very good hopper. She doesn't enjoy being ill and is afraid of certain sounds. Pretending is fun for this child, as is roughhousing with her older brother.

IL: Ages 4-6

6.12 Fitzhugh, Louise. **I Am Three.** New York: Delacorte Press, 1982. 43 pp.

A three-year old girl declares that she likes to make friends, likes herself, and likes presents. She is particular about her meals and doesn't want others to receive any attention when she's around. The little girl's sleeping habits are also described--she fights falling asleep, enjoys hearing a story, carries a blanket, and wakes up very early.

IL: Ages 2-4

6.13 Frankel. **Once Upon a Potty.** see Ch. 8.

6.14 Girard, Linda. **You Were Born on Your Very First Birthday.** Chicago: Albert Whitman and Company, 1983. 29 pp.

A baby's development within the comfortable mother's womb is described. Movements the developing baby is capable of and its great change in size during the nine months are stressed. The baby is described as being restless and ready for a change of surroundings at birth, at which time it is welcomed by its new parents.

IL: Ages 4-6

6.15 Greenberg. **I Know I'm Myself Because...** see Ch. 8.

6.16 Greenberg. **What Is the Sign for Friend?** see Ch. 10.

6.17 Harris. **I Hate Kisses.** see Ch. 3.

6.18 Henkes. **Clean Enough.** see Ch. 8.

6.19 Hines. **All By Myself.** see Ch. 8.

6.20 Hoopes, Lyn. **When I Was Little.** New York: E.P. Dutton, 1983. 27 pp.

During a walk on a snowy day with her mother carrying baby brother in a pack, a young girl questions her mother about events in the past. Her mother patiently and lovingly explains the parents' excitement during pregnancy, the joyous occasion of her birth, and the parents' amazement as she grew and learned. Just as the girl once fit snugly in the pack, her baby brother does now.

IL: Ages 4-6

6.21 Horner, Althea. **Little Big Girl.** New York: Human Sciences Press, 1983. 30 pp.

Although five-and-a-half year old Mary Ellen enjoys having more privileges and responsibilities, she fears that her parents won't love her as much now that she's a big girl. The attention received by a new baby cousin only intensifies Mary Ellen's worries and she requests that her parents dress and feed her once again. When her parents discover what's troubling Mary Ellen, they reassure her that she'll never be too big for hugs and kisses and lots of attention from them.

IL: Ages 4-6

6.22 Jonas, Ann. **When You Were a Baby.** New York: Greenwillow Books, 1982. 22 pp.

Compared to infancy, a young child is reminded of the many abilities now possessed such as piling blocks, pulling a wagon, using a spoon and glass, rolling a ball, and so on.

IL: Ages 2-4

6.23 Keller. **Too Big.** see Ch. 4.

6.24 Kent, Jack. **Knee-High Nina.** Garden City, NY: Doubleday and Company, 1980. 29 pp.

Tired of always seeing the bottom of things and asking grownups to obtain objects from high shelves for her, small Nina wishes to grow to the size of an adult. When her wish comes true, Nina takes advantage of her height but finds she must now help out her tiny parents. Holding her tiny mother on her lap, Nina declares that being big is not as much fun as she thought. Wishing she could wait a while before growing up, Nina becomes child sized once again.

IL: Ages 2-4

6.25 McDaniel, Becky. **Katie Couldn't.** Chicago: Children's Press, 1985. 30 pp.

Young Katie is unhappy because she can't ride a bike, stay up late, or walk to the park like her older sister and brother are capable of doing. Wishing she were bigger, Katie discovers that while her older siblings are too big for dad to pick up and toss in the air, Katie is just the right size.

IL: Ages 2-4

6.26 McPhail. **Andrew's Bath.** see Ch. 5.

6.27 Moncure, Jane. **NOW I AM FIVE!** Chicago: Children's Press, 1984. 31 pp.

A five-year old girl displays her new skills--skipping, roller skating, riding a bike, as well as helping at home by making her bed and caring for a pet. She especially enjoys kindergarten activities and her ability to count, print her name, and tie her shoes.

IL: Ages 4-6

6.28 Moncure, Jane. **NOW I AM FOUR!** Chicago: Children's Press, 1984. 31 pp.

A four-year old takes pride in newly acquired dressing skills and physical accomplishments at the playground. The child also enjoys art activities, pretending, looking at books, and playing games with friends.

IL: Ages 4-6

6.29 Moncure, Jane. **NOW I AM THREE!** Chicago: Children's Press, 1984. 31 pp.

Climbing, zipping a jacket, helping mother shop, playing make-believe--these are all achievements a three-year old girl proudly demonstrates. She is also shown at a nursery school participating in various independent and group activities.

IL: Ages 2-4

6.30 Moncure, Jane. **NOW I AM TWO!** Chicago: Children's Press, 1984. 31 pp.

A two-year old describes important accomplishments; the child is now able to run, jump, do puzzles, pedal a trike, make a block train, etc. Certain dressing and bathroom skills are also a source of pride for the child.

IL: Ages 2-4

6.31 Parish. **I Can-Can You?** see Ch. 8.

6.32 Sheffield, Margaret. **Before You Were Born.** New York: Alfred A. Knopf, 1984. 31 pp.

A glimpse of a developing baby's life in the womb is compared to activities a young child is capable of. Swimming underwater, kicking, and hearing sounds are all discussed as a part of growth. The birth experience is also described.

IL: Ages 4-6

6.33 Stanovich, Betty. **Big Boy, Little Boy.** New York: Lothrop, Lee, and Shepard, 1984. 27 pp.

Grandma is busy so David needs to build with blocks and draw to keep himself entertained. While praising his abilities, Grandma reminds David of the many things he could not do when he was little that he is capable of now. To help him remember his younger self, Grandma also sings to David and tells him a story while rocking him to sleep.

IL: Ages 4-6

6.34 Szekeres, Cyndy. **Puppy Too Small.** Racine, WI: Western Publishing, 1984. 14 pp.

Puppy laments the fact that he is too small to reach the doorknob, pull his toy box, and climb a tree. However, there are many things he can do; he can reach the cookie plate, pull a small wagon, and swing from the tree. That evening Puppy's mother lists his accomplishments for the day and mentions that he is just the right size for a hug.

IL: Ages 2-4

6.35 Szekeres. **Thumpity Thump Gets Dressed.** see Ch. 8.

6.36 Walsh. **Theodore All Grown Up.** see Ch. 8.

6.37 Thomson, Ruth and Ian Beck. **My Bear: I Can...Can You?** New York: E.P. Dutton, 1985. 27 pp.

A small bear demonstrates prowess at standing on one leg, fixing toys that break, writing, counting, throwing a ball, tying shoelaces, and so on.

IL: Ages 2-4

6.38 Watanabe, Shigeo. **Get set! Go!** New York: G.P. Putnam's Sons, 1981. 28 pp.

A young bear has problems with each part of an obstacle race, yet he perseveres. His only concern is the thrill he feels as he crosses the finish line.

IL: Ages 2-4

6.39 Watanabe. **How do I put it on?** see Ch. 8.

6.40 Watanabe, Shigeo. **I can ride it.** New York: G.P. Putnam's Sons, 1981. 28 pp.

Wanting to keep up with his older friends, a young bear progresses from tricycle riding to roller skates and a two-wheeler with training wheels. The bear struggles to do his best and makes compensations when needed.

IL: Ages 2-4

6.41 Ziefert, Harriet. **diggity dig!** New York: Viking Press, 1984. 14 pp.

A boy and girl demonstrate their abilities to bounce a ball, push, slide, climb, etc.

IL: Ages 2-4

6.42 Ziefert. **zippety zip!** see Ch. 8.

7

Peers and School

Children from the ages of two to six learn how to make social contacts and how to get along with people outside the family, especially children their own age. They learn to adapt themselves to others and to cooperate with other children during play activity. Studies on preschool children suggest that the social attitudes and behaviors established during these early years often persist with little change as children grow older. The early-childhood period has been appropriately labeled the "pregang age." Obviously during the years from two to six, the peer group does not have the influence on children that it does at later stages of development. However, contact with other children during the early stages of development does indeed have an impact on the child's social and emotional development. For example, children who attend day-care or nursery school, provided these are of high quality, often show better emotional and social adjustment than those children who do not have similar experiences. Even though it is clear that the peer group is critical to a child's development and that a preschool experience can enhance the growth process, there are a number of important issues that one should be aware of concerning these two social components.

Peer Relationships

During the years from two to six, children first begin to show an active interest in the peer group. The peer group offers a number of important functions for the growth and development of children. One particularly important function of the peer group for children is to facilitate play.

General functions of the peer group. Preschool children spend a considerable amount of time with their peers. These experiences can create much happiness for children and frustration as well. Naturally, children do best when interacting with children of similar age; however, it is not unusual for children to play with others three or four years younger or older. As parents and professionals often realize, children may be of different chronological age; however, their emotional and behavioral maturity may be similar(1). For example, the six-year-old child may find much more satisfaction in a peer group of four-year-old children than with other six-year-olds.

A number of studies have shown the influence of the peer

group on young children. For example, Anna Freud found in her classic study of six children who banded together after their parents were killed in World War II that they survived through their attachment to each other(2). Even though these children were deprived of parental care, they became neither emotionally troubled nor delinquent.

Other studies have reported that both positive and negative peer interaction increases throughout the early-childhood period. Even though aggressive interaction and rough-and-tumble play increase during peer group interaction, children gradually acquire more mature methods of relating to peers with the passage of time. At times aggressive behavior even during the early stages of child development cannot be allowed to evolve through its natural course and adults must intervene. Consequently, there are negative aspects of peer interaction that suggest peer group activities must be monitored by parents and others.

Clearly the peer group serves a number of general functions for preschool children. Even though peer interaction does not have the same significance for the younger child as the older child, it should be kept in mind, nonetheless, that the peer group is a necessity for the development of all children.

One of the most elaborate attempts to examine play of preschool children was done by Mildred Parten(3). Her research was conducted in a nursery school. She used an observational method and developed six categories of play indicative of children in a group setting.

Unoccupied play. This is the least common kind of play in a group setting. The child does not engage in play as it is commonly understood and appears to perform random movements and activities that appear to have no goal to them.

Solitary play. The child plays independently and seems to be highly engrossed in play, paying little or no attention to others. The two- and three-year-old child most often engages in solitary play. As children mature, they are less apt to engage in this play.

Onlooker. The child takes an active interest in the play of others by watching them. The child may talk to other children playing, but does not enter into their play. The child's active interest in others who are at play distinguishes this form of play from unoccupied play.

Parallel play. The child plays alone, but with toys that are similar to those of other children at play. The children mimic each other in behavior but there is no interaction suggesting the children are playing with each other. Older children are less likely to be involved in parallel play.

Associative play. This kind of play is not highly organized but does involve interaction. Children engage in play with others; however, the important ingredient appears to be that they be associated with other children and not necessarily be involved in tasks that require association to be accomplished. During associative play, children will borrow or lend toys and follow or lead each other; however, individual children will generally play as they wish and the group is of secondary importance.

Cooperative play. This form of play requires group interaction. The group develops a sense of identity and activity is organized. Competition aimed at winning something and formal games are examples of cooperative play. This kind of play is a prototype for the games so important to middle childhood and later development.

Keith Barnes in a more recent study observed preschoolers using Parten's categories and did indeed find that children continue to play in a similar fashion; however, there was some decrease in associative and cooperative play(4). One should be aware that the kinds of play described by Parten, and later studied by Keith Barnes, are ways in which developing children interact at one time or another. Each of these kinds of play is important to social and emotional development. It should be noted that each kind of play is more indicative of various stages within early-childhood development. For example, a child who is two years old should not be expected to interact with peers in cooperative play. Obviously, the two-year-old has not developed the emotional and behavioral skills required for this kind of play. Keeping such issues in mind, the preschool child receives important peer group interaction through play and this activity should be supported and nurtured.

The School Experience

Many women today must return to work almost immediately after giving birth. Research generally suggests that most women with children cannot afford to stay at home and must contribute to the family income. Many other women have demanding careers that they do not want to abandon. Parents face a difficult task when trying to arrange a safe and reliable environment for their children while they work. Some parents are able to hire relatives or friends to watch their children; others must rely upon day-care or nursery school. Presently in American society there is some concern about the impact that substitute care has on preschool children. Placing a child in substitute care can be a trying experience for not only the child, but also the parent. Even if the child does not experience substitute care during early-childhood, the child must ultimately go to kindergarten. This is also a major transition point in the child's life that can be quite stressful.

A number of studies have been conducted on day-care settings for children. The general theme of this research suggests that if day-care is well run and is of high quality, parents should have little fear of the day-care experience negatively impacting the child(5). The authors recently conducted a very thorough review of the literature on the impact of day-care on children, as well as their families, and made the following conclusions:

1. For children of advantaged backgrounds, studies have generally found no differences in intellectual development, as measured mainly by standardized tests, between home reared children and those experiencing day-care. For high-risk children (i.e., those from low income families), day-care appears to have a positive impact on their intellectual development.

2. With a few exceptions, studies have not found major differences in mother-child attachment between children reared at home and those reared in day-care. This suggests that day-care does not have a negative impact on a child's emotional development.

3. Day-care appears to impact a child's social development. Compared to home reared children, those children experiencing day-care seem to be more peer oriented and less likely to interact with adults. Behavioral differences related to aggression, assertiveness, and cooperation were also found between home reared and day-care children.

4. Some evidence suggests that day-care has a positive impact on the family system in terms of family income and several other significant factors such as mothers earning a high school degree and higher wages.

It is estimated that by 1990, 75 percent of women with children will work outside the home(6). It is evident that substitute care, in particular day-care, is a service that families currently need and will continue to need. It is also evident that when preschool children enter a substitute care setting, this process is stressful for the child as well as for the parent. For example, most children have no trouble coping with multiple attachments; they generally form close attachments to their teachers. If they have a choice between mother and teacher, however, they usually prefer their mothers. Even though most children can cope with the issue of multiple attachments, it does not mean that the process of learning to deal with such arrangements is without stress for the child and parent. There are some fairly predictable patterns that normally emerge when a child enters day-care or even kindergarten.

Starting school. Starting to go to day-care or kindergarten is a new experience for a child; teachers realize this and so do many parents. There are ways in which both parents and teachers can minimize the tension for the child. One important step is to make sure the first day is brief and that the parent is highly involved, as well as the new caretakers. Little or no activity should be planned for the child such as group play and so on.

With the cooperation of the parents, teachers in the new school setting can gradually introduce children to life in their new environment. Trained staff try to get to know each child during the first weeks of school and learn about each child's background; this helps teachers guide children in their adjustment to school. Most children adjust well, and there are no long term effects. However, for almost all children, the process does involve change and the learning of new behaviors. Some children do not adjust as well as others and special problems may arise; this calls for patience from teachers and parents alike in helping such children gradually learn to cope with their new environment.

Often quality schools provide a cubby for each child's belongings. This cubby gives a child a sense of individual identity within the new school setting as well as a place of refuge when the going is rough. Many preschool children seem to be able to face the strangeness of a nursery school or kindergarten environment if they are accompanied to school by a favorite teddy bear or other stuffed animal or doll.

As children begin to accept school, they gain confidence in the self and gradually learn to interact with other children. This interaction is an important source of play for the child. The child learns the meaning of cooperation with others; such lessons are a necessity for successful living in later years(7). The child entering a school setting also learns physical and emotional self-control, among other important psychological activities.

Adjusting to school. Children typically adjust to their new school setting in gauche and crude ways. Some children feel amiable but are not aware of ways to express the self. Aggression is normal for some children who are afraid of and uncertain about their new environment. Other children have to learn how to defend the self almost as often as the child needs to be kept from fighting. As children learn to adjust, they gradually resolve their battles with little or no interference by teachers. Certain children will use temper tantrums as a device to get attention. In other words, there are a number of ways children react to day-care or kindergarten; this is all part of the adjustment process(8).

Children who have been over-controlled at home will probably have problems in initiating activities with other children. Some children will be anxious and fearful until they are helped to resolve their negative feelings. Other children will withdraw into themselves and show little or no interest in others. Trained staff are aware that all of these behaviors are the ways that children initially cope with the new school setting. Parents should be particularly attuned to these predictable ways of coping for children. Parents and teacher, by working together in both the home and the substitute care setting, can help children adjust to their new environment. It must be kept in mind that substitute care is a necessity for many families and that such care can support the emotional and social development of children.

Peers and School in Early
  Childhood Literature

Almost every aspect of friendship is explored in various picture books about the ups and downs of relationships: learning to share, planning projects, being jealous, having a quarrel, exchanging confidences, and above all, having fun(9). During the early-childhood years, most children make their first ventures outside the home to play with friends their own age and are interested in hearing about characters in books doing the same. The companionship and squabbles of two- and three-year-olds engaged in parallel play are depicted in books for preschoolers. Likewise, the more sophisticated associative play and perhaps a hint of organized cooperative play is shown in books for the child approaching six years of age. The very real emotions of sadness and loneliness that accompany a friend's moving away are also the subject of many books for the older preschool child.

Preschool children are often faced with a school situation as a setting for social and emotional development as well. As more and more children participate in programs at kindergartens, nursery schools, day-care centers, or less formal group programs, the need for books that will prepare them for such experiences becomes clear(10). Many books, with as much focus on good illustrations as words, depict the activities and routine that a young child can expect from a day-care or nursery school setting. Starting kindergarten, the first school experience for some children and a major transition even for those who have gone to day-care, has been the subject of many excellent books as well. No matter what the age of the preschool child, it is no doubt comforting to see book characters who find it difficult to separate from their mothers, who may resist the sudden need to follow a routine designed for a group, and who may not be able to easily make new friends at school.

Responses to the literature. Books depicting preschool characters who make forays outside the home to the world of peers and school should draw a favorable response from most two- to six-year-olds. As many preschool children spend an increasing amount of time with agemates in day-care or nursery school settings, it appears essential for these children to be able to identify with book characters in the same situation. The child experiencing school adjustment problems or friendship problems can probably come up with possible solutions to these troubles after hearing about a preschooler in the literature who faces a similar challenge.

Early-childhood books concerning peers and school could often be read aloud to a group of children, with certain children probably more than willing to share similar experiences they've had. A preschool child who has more individual needs may wish to hear such reassuring stories alone. Whether books on peers and school are used with a group or an individual, the adult guide may want to choose to extend responses to the literature by using these or other related follow-up activities:

1. Creating puppets to dramatize a child and a friend involved in play or settling a conflict.
2. Drawing or painting by the child of a favorite snack at school or an activity that the child enjoys at school.
3. Charting the child's daily schedule, complete with pictures or photographs, making sure that time spent with parents, time at nursery school, and time spent with friends are all included.
4. Having the child supply a friend's name for statements such as: _____ has nice parents. _____ is fun to eat lunch with. _____ likes to play make-believe with me. _____ fights with me.
5. Encouraging two children to role play best friends involved in play, with a third child approaching them and asking to be included(11).

The socialization of the child, which begins with the family, ultimately includes peers and the school. How relationships with friends and those with teachers and agemates at school are different from those developed within the family system is a topic explored by many picture books written for the preschool child. The family is still a backdrop for most of these stories, yet they focus on the child's developmental needs to socialize and gradually gain some independence. It appears that the reading of such books by an adult guide, followed by a child's personal input, could facilitate social and emotional growth in the preschool child.

NOTES

1. William W. Hartup, "Peer Interaction and the Development of the Individual Child," in Eric Schopler and Robert Reichler (eds.), Psychopathology and Child Development (New York: Plenum, 1976), p. 10.

2. Anna Freud, War and Children 2d ed., edited by Philip R. Lehrman (New York: International University Press, 1944).

3. Mildred Parten, "Social Play Among Preschool Children," Journal of Abnormal and Social Psychology (Volume XXVII, 1932): 243-269.

4. Keith E. Barnes, "Preschool Play Norms: A Replication," Developmental Psychology (Volume V, No. 1, 1971): 99-103.

5. John T. Pardeck and Jean A. Pardeck, "The Impact of Day Care on the Preschool Child: Research Findings and Implications," International Social Work (Volume XXVIII, No. 3, 1985): 40-48.

6. Edward F. Zigler and Edmund W. Gordon (eds.), Day Care: Scientific and Social Policy Issues (Boston: Auburn House, 1982), pp. v-vi.

7. Elizabeth B. Hurlock, Child Development 6th ed. (New York: McGraw-Hill, 1978), p. 238.

8. Hurlock, p. 239.

9. Zena Sutherland, Dianne Monson, and May Hill Arbuthnot, Children and Books 6th ed. (Glenview, Illinois: Scott, Foresman, and Company, 1981), p. 108.

10. Sutherland, Monson, and Arbuthnot, p. 108.

11. Don Dinkmeyer, Developing Understanding of Self and Others (DUSO) Manual (Circle Pines, Minnesota: American Guidance Service, 1970); Jean A. Pardeck and John T. Pardeck, Young People with Problems: A Guide to Bibliotherapy (Westport, Connecticut: Greenwood Press, 1984); Ellen Weiss, Sesame Street—My Memory Book (New York: Children's Television Workshop, 1983).

BOOKS

7.1 Adams. **The Scaredy Book.** see Ch. 5.

7.2 Alexander, Martha. **Move Over, Twerp.** New York: The Dial Press, 1981. 28 pp.

When his mother announces he's old enough to ride the bus, young Jeffrey is thrilled until older children start to harass him on the way to school. Although Jeffrey's father and older sister both give him advice on dealing with his predicament, Jeffrey himself comes up with the best idea to handle the situation. With some imagination and a sense of humor, Jeffrey is able to once again enjoy his bus ride to school.

IL: Ages 4-6

7.3 Alexander, Martha. **We're in Big Trouble, Blackboard Bear.** New York: The Dial Press, 1980. 30 pp.

Anthony's imaginary bear is accused of taking the belongings of Anthony's friends. The bear admits later to Anthony that he did sneak out at night and take their possessions, but he was afraid to tell because Anthony might stop liking him. Anthony assures the bear he'll always be his friend and the two make plans to apologize and replace the items.

IL: Ages 4-6

7.4 Barbato. **From Bed to Bus.** see Ch. 8.

7.5 Bottner. **Mean Maxine.** see Ch. 2.

7.6 Brandenberg, Aliki. **We Are Best Friends.** New York: Greenwillow Books, 1982. 28 pp.

In despair when his best friend Peter moves away, Robert claims there will be no one to play with or to fight with. Peter writes a letter to Robert describing his new home and school; he mentions a new friend but states that Robert is still his best friend. Although it's a bit harder for Robert to develop a new friendship, he eventually writes to Peter about a new friend he has met as well.

IL: Ages 4-6

7.7 Bruna, Dick. **Miffy Goes to School.** Los Angeles: Price, Stern, and Sloan, 1984. 26 pp.

A pleasant school day for Miffy the rabbit is described. Arrival at school, drawing, working with numbers, singing, and play with blocks are all activities making up the little rabbit's routine. The day ends with storytime and a warm good-bye from the teacher.

IL: Ages 4-6

7.8 Calmenson, Stephanie. **The Kindergarten Book.** New York: Grosset and Dunlap, 1983. 45 pp.

A collection of four stories about animal characters attending kindergarten describes: 1) students getting accustomed to the classroom routine and being away from their mothers, 2) a student's problem with learning the difference between left and right, 3) a student's realization that being small can have advantages, and 4) students developing a friendly relationship with their principal.

IL: Ages 4-6

7.9 Cooney. **The Blanket that Had to Go.** see Ch. 8.

7.10 Corey. **Everybody Take Turns.** see Ch. 3.

7.11 Corey. **We All Share.** see Ch. 3.

7.12 Corrigan. **Emily Umily.** see Ch. 10.

7.13 Counsel. **But Martin!** see Ch. 3.

7.14 Crary. **I Can't Wait.** see Ch. 3.

7.15 Crary, Elizabeth. **I Want It.** Seattle: Parenting Press, 1982. 30 pp.

Two girls, who are playmates, have problems when one girl wants the other's toy. The child wanting the toy can think of several ways to solve her problem--grabbing the toy, threatening to go home, making a deal with the other child, getting help from a parent, asking for the toy, or waiting for a turn. Discussion questions are included to help children explore the possible outcome of each of the above approaches to solving this problem situation.

IL: Ages 4-6

7.16 Crary. **I Want to Play.** see Ch. 3.

7.17 Crary, Elizabeth. **My Name is not Dummy.** Seattle: Parenting Press, 1983. 30 pp.

When a boy and girl who are usually friends have a quarrel, the boy begins name-calling. The other child explores several alternatives to deal with her anger at being called a name. Her choices include crying or calling him a name also, neither of which would help much, as well as ignoring the name-calling or asking why he is mad, perhaps better choices. This book includes questions for an adult to use in starting a discussion with children about different ways to respond to a conflict such as this.

IL: Ages 4-6

7.18 Davis. **The Other Emily.** see Ch. 8.

7.19 Delton, Judy. **Lee Henry's Best Friend.** Chicago: Albert Whitman and Company, 1980. 28 pp.

Having found a best friend with lots of good qualities and many shared interests, Lee Henry is very upset when his friend's family has to move away. The two boys promise to write, send pictures, and be best friends forever. Although Lee Henry's mother encourages him to look for another friend, Lee Henry refuses until a new boy on the block seeks him out.

IL: Ages 4-6

7.20 Dickinson, Mary. **Alex and Roy.** London: Andre Deutsch, 1981. 29 pp.

When Roy comes to visit Alex, Alex declares he doesn't want to play and hides in his room. Alex's mother wisely keeps Roy occupied until a curious Alex emerges to join in the fun. Alex and Roy spend a happy morning in a car made of boxes pretending they are going to the train station, grandmother's house, a beauty shop, and even Africa. Alex even wishes Roy could stay longer when his mother arrives to take him home.

IL: Ages 4-6

7.21 Dickinson, Mary. **Alex's Outing.** London: Andre Deutsch, 1983. 30 pp.

Alex and his friends are excited about an outing to the country with their mothers where they run, play in the mud, eat a picnic lunch, and pick blackberries. One mother scolds her daughter for running, being noisy, and getting dirty, so Alex worries that his mom may be cross about his stained clothing and torn jeans. Alex's mother, however, is very tolerant of messy children and is simply pleased that the two of them had such a good time.

IL: Ages 4-6

7.22 Dinan. **The Lunch Box Monster.** see Ch. 5.

7.23 Edwards, Dorothy and Shirley Hughes. **My Naughty Little Sister and Bad Harry's Rabbit.** Englewood Cliffs, NJ: Prentice-Hall, 1981. 23 pp.

When Bad Harry receives a pair of too-small shoes, a friend has the idea of putting the shoes on his stuffed rabbit so it can stand up. Harry and his friend are photographed with the stuffed rabbit during a shopping trip; however, Harry does not appear in the picture in the newspaper. Only Harry's friend is able to make him feel better when she discovers why.

IL: Ages 4-6

7.24 Eriksson. **Jealousy.** see Ch. 2.

7.25 Frandsen, Karen. I **Started School Today.** Chicago: Children's Press, 1984. 31 pp.

In describing the first day of school, a young child tells of mothers bringing their children to school, some children crying or wanting to go home, the class making behavior rules, the children having a snack, etc. A very patient teacher keeps her sense of humor during a couple of unexpected events. Riding home on the bus, the child and a new friend consider running away to avoid school, but the child decides to check in at home and think about the next school day instead.

IL: Ages 4-6

7.26 Gantz, David. **First Day at School.** New York: Crown Publishers, 1984. 31 pp.

Although his two bunny siblings are eager to start their first day at school, Three O'Hare has to be coaxed by his mother to dress and eat breakfast. Convinced that he will hate school, Three O'Hare is not reassured by his mother or his kind-looking teacher. However, once he becomes involved with block play, story time, painting, etc., Three O'Hare discovers that he enjoys kindergarten and is the first one ready for the school bus the next day.

IL: Ages 4-6

7.27 Greenberg. **What Is the Sign for Friend?** see Ch. 10.

7.28 Guzzo, Sandra. **Fox and Heggie.** Chicago: Albert Whitman and Company, 1983. 29 pp.

When his friend Fox decides to save money for a cap he admires, Heggie the hedgehog offers Fox his coins as well. Fox does odd jobs all week, only to lose his money on the way to buy the cap. A forlorn Fox goes to eat at Heggie's house, where he discovers a surprise party where all his friends have purchased the cap for him.

IL: Ages 4-6

7.29 Hamilton-Merritt, Jane. **My First Days of School.** New York: Julian Messner, 1982. 25 pp.

With the encouragement of a very supportive family, five year old Kate and her teddy bear attend the first day of kindergarten. Kate has a busy day full of new activities and classroom rules to remember. During her second day of school, Kate befriends a new girl and a shy boy and decides she no longer needs to be accompanied by her teddy bear.

IL: Ages 4-6

7.30 Hayes, Geoffrey. **Patrick and Ted.** New York: Four Winds Press, 1984. 26 pp.

Best friends Patrick and Ted are almost like brothers and are always thought of as a pair. Therefore, when Ted leaves for the summer, Patrick is reluctant to begin playing with other friends and finds he must entertain himself at times. Upon Ted's return, the two friends quarrel. Although they make up and spend much time together once again, their relationship is no longer exclusive of other friends.

IL: Ages 4-6

7.31 Hazen. **Very Shy.** see Ch. 2.

7.32 Heine, Helme. **Friends.** New York: Atheneum, 1982. 28 pp.

Charlie Rooster, Johnny Mouse, and Percy the pig, who are very good friends, spend the day bicycling around the countryside. They illustrate and describe characteristics of good friends--sticking together, deciding things together, being fair, etc. After attempting unsuccessfully to spend the night with each other, the three friends discover that they can't always be together, yet they can think about and dream about each other when they're apart.

IL: Ages 4-6

7.33 Hickman, Martha. **The Reason I'm Not Quite Finished Tying My Shoes.** Nashville: Abingdon, 1981. 25 pp.

Unsure of whether she wants to go to school that day, Annamaria thinks up different reasons why she can't tie her shoes. Her socks are too pretty to cover up; her toes might itch; her shoes might be too small. With her mother ready to leave for work, Annamaria explains the real reason she hasn't tied her shoes--she can't find them.

IL: Ages 4-6

7.34 Hill, Eric. **Spot Goes to School.** New York: G.P. Putnam's Sons, 1984. 22 pp.

On his first day of school, Spot the puppy plays dress-up, uses blocks, participates in Show 'n Tell, and has fun on the playground with other animal friends. Although he hides during singing time and emerges from school covered with paint, Spot proclaims to his mother that school was "Great!"

IL: Ages 2-4

7.35 Hines. **Bethany for Real.** see Ch. 5.

7.36 Hines. **Maybe a Band-Aid Will Help.** see Ch. 4.

7.37 Jackson, Kim. **First Day of School.** Mahwah, NJ: Troll Associates, 1985. 28 pp.

Dressed in new clothes and shoes, Cindy the mouse is eager to accompany her mother on the way to her first day of school. Everything looks big to Cindy--the school building, the hallway, the classroom door, and her teacher, causing Cindy to suddenly feel shy. However, once Cindy begins drawing pictures, she makes a new friend and her first day at school seems terrific.

IL: Ages 4-6

7.38 Kaye, Marilyn. **Will You Cross Me?** New York: Harper and Row, 1985. 32 pp.

Two friends living on opposite sides of the street, Joe and Sam, have problems getting together to play. They try throwing a ball across the street for a while. Once they are on the same side of the street, Joe and Sam have a dispute about how to play ball. When Joe and Sam finally agree on sharing the ball and bat, Joe's mother calls for him to come in the house.

IL: Ages 4-6

7.39 Maestro, Betsy and Giulio. **Harriet at School.** New York: Crown Publishers, 1984. 11 pp.

Harriet the elephant spends a day at school painting, having a snack, playing dress-up, singing at music time, listening to a story, etc. She loves her school and teacher and enjoys playing with friends there.

IL: Ages 2-4

7.40 Muntean, Michaela. **I Like School.** Racine, WI: Western Publishing Company, 1980. 24 pp.

The Sesame Street characters very simply describe what they like about school during the course of a school day. Included are music, snacktime, the teacher, the playground, and riding home on the bus.

IL: Ages 2-6

7.41 O'Brien, Anne. **Come Play with Us.** New York: Holt, Rinehart, and Winston, 1985. 14 pp.

When her father takes her to day-care, Rachel is sad to see him leave. She soon gets involved playing with two children and eats lunch with two other friends. Knowing her father would come back for her, Rachel is reassured nonetheless when he picks her up from day-care.

IL: Ages 2-4

7.42 O'Brien. **I Want That!** see Ch. 3.

7.43 Oxenbury. **The Birthday Party.** see Ch. 2.

7.44 Oxenbury, Helen. **First Day of School.** New York: E.P. Dutton, 1983. 16 pp.

A little girl is hesitant to attend her first day of nursery school, so her mother stays with her a while until she meets a new friend. The little girl is shown participating in teacher-led activities, as well as eating snacks and using the bathroom. She runs to her mother when it's time to go home.

IL: Ages 2-4

7.45 Panek. **Matilda Hippo Has a Big Mouth.** see Ch. 3.

7.46 Poulet, Virginia. **Blue Bug Goes to School.** Chicago: Children's Press, 1985. 32 pp.

Blue Bug demonstrates a variety of learning activities at school. These include learning the alphabet, writing his name, and counting as well as drawing, cutting, and using clay.

IL: Ages 2-6

7.47 Rabe. **The Balancing Girl.** see Ch. 10.

7.48 Rogers, Fred. **Going to Day Care.** New York: G.P. Putnam's Sons, 1985. 27 pp.

The care a child receives at a day care center is compared to being taken care of at home by parents. The conflict of being in a new situation away from parents is discussed, as well as the excitement and fun of day care activities such as painting, hearing stories, having new playthings, and making friends. It is stressed that children must learn to share and to wait at times at day care centers. The end of the day brings a reunion with parents who are proud of the child's growing independence and new accomplishments.

IL: Ages 2-6

7.49 Rosenberg. **My Friend Leslie: The Story of a Handicapped Child.** see Ch. 10.

7.50 Ryder, Eileen. **Winklet Goes to School.** New York: Burke Books, 1982. 23 pp.

On her first day at school, Winklet clings to her mother and cries when she leaves. Children in her class offer her toys, but she pushes them away until one child holds out a doll to her. After holding the doll, Winklet joins in the sand play, painting, and storytime. When her mother comes, Winklet waves good-bye and promises to come back the next day.

IL: Ages 2-6

7.51 Schwartz. **Bea and Mr. Jones.** see Ch. 8.

7.52 Sellers, Ronnie. **My First Day at School.** New York: Caedmon, 1985. 29 pp.

A little boy is apprehensive about his first day of school until his mother promises to come along and shows him his new lunch box and schoolbag. Once there, a friendly teacher shows him his desk, has his class tell their names, and asks what the class wants to learn that year. Lunchtime arrives quickly, followed by a busy afternoon. The little boy leaves for home proud that he had such a successful first day.

IL: Ages 4-6

7.53 Sharmat. **Atilla the Angry.** see Ch. 2.

7.54 Sharmat. **Bartholomew the Bossy.** see Ch. 3.

7.55 Sharmat. **Grumley the Grouch.** see Ch. 2.

7.56 Sharmat, Marjorie. **Rollo and Juliet, Forever!** Garden City, NY: Doubleday and Company, 1981. 29 pp.

Two cats, Rollo and Juliet, are best friends until Rollo decides to become acquainted with a new cat in the neighborhood. A quarrel follows; the two friends avoid one another; and they are not on speaking terms for two weeks. After one misguided attempt to make up, Rollo and Juliet agree to meet only so they can discuss all the things they dislike about one another. Once the air is cleared, the two decide to try being friends once again.

IL: Ages 4-6

7.57 Sharmat, Marjorie. **Taking Care of Melvin.** New York: Holiday House, 1980. 28 pp.

Melvin Dog spends so much time being generous and performing thoughtful deeds for his friends, he has no time for himself. When Melvin becomes ill and must rest in bed, he becomes overbearing in the demands he makes on his friends. His friends realize how they have overworked Melvin in the past and once he is well, they ask him to just be their friend and take care of himself.

IL: Ages 4-6

7.58 Sharmat. **Twitchell the Wishful.** see Ch. 2.

7.59 Snyder, Zilpha. **Come On, Patsy.** New York: Atheneum, 1982. 32 pp.

When Patsy's bossy friend encourages her to go to the park, trouble begins. Following her friend's advice leads to Patsy's dress being torn, her knee getting hurt, her shoes getting muddy, and Patsy getting sick after riding a merry-go-round. Although Patsy's father is quite angry when the two girls arrive home, her bossy friend can't understand why Patsy refuses to play the next day.

IL: Ages 4-6

7.60 Soderstrom, Mary. **Maybe Tomorrow I'll Have a Good Time.** New York: Human Sciences Press, 1981. 27 pp.

Accustomed to being at home with her mother, Marsha Lou is apprehensive about going to a day care center when her mother starts a new job. Preparing for Marsha Lou's first day at the day care center, her mother keeps emphasizing how big Marsha Lou is now. During her first day, Marsha Lou is comforted by the teacher when she cries and is allowed to just observe the other children having fun with different activities. When her mother arrives to take her home, Marsha Lou declares she was mad and sad most of the day, but feels she might have a better time tomorrow.

IL: Ages 4-6

7.61 Stanek, Muriel. **Starting School.** Chicago: Albert Whitman and Company, 1981. 30 pp.

A little boy's parents wisely prepare him for school--he visits the building and meets his teacher, learns his address and phone number, goes to the doctor for a checkup, and shops for new shoes. His first day at school is filled with activities such as drawing pictures, hearing a story, singing, and writing his name. The little boy makes a friend and is happy to see his mother at the end of the schoolday.

IL: Ages 4-6

7.62 Tobias, Tobi. **The Dawdlewalk.** Minneapolis: Carolrhoda Books, 1983. 27 pp.

During his morning walk to school, a young boy stops to watch the birds, talk to people, look in the store windows, etc. Claiming he will never arrive at school on time, the boy's mother urges him to quit dawdling. Only when his mother stops to chat with a friend, does the boy suddenly express an urgency to get to school.

IL: Ages 4-6

7.63 Warren, Cathy. **Fred's First Day.** New York: Lothrop, Lee, and Shepard, 1984. 31 pp.

Too small to do things with his older brother and too big to play with his baby brother, middle child Fred often feels left out. Fred's wise mother enrolls him in nursery school with children just his size, but the boys and girls there don't seem to want to play with him that first morning either. At playtime, however, Fred comforts two crying children and is accepted by his classmates. He is glad to see his mother when school's over and explains to baby brother how he will one day be just the right size to attend school.

IL: Ages 4-6

7.64 Watts, Marjorie-Ann. **Zebra Goes to School.** London: Andre Deutsch, 1981. 31 pp.

Reluctant to begin school, Jimmy takes his Zebra playmate along the first day. Although no one else can see the zebra, Jimmy is kept busy that first day helping Zebra to overcome his shyness and get adjusted to classroom activities. Zebra seems unhappy with the first few days of school, wanting only to play outside and disliking lunch, while Jimmy finds himself enjoying school. At last Jimmy declares he doesn't need Zebra's companionship anymore and decides to leave Zebra at home with his baby brother.

IL: Ages 4-6

7.65 Weiss. **The Angry Book.** see Ch. 2.

7.66 Wells, Rosemary. **Timothy Goes to School.** New York: The Dial Press, 1981. 28 pp.

Young Timothy feels left out during his first week of school and doesn't want to go anymore. One of his classmates has all the friends and seems to be the smartest and best at everything. When Timothy meets a girl who shares his feelings about school, the two become friends and forget their troubles.

IL: Ages 4-6

7.67 Winthrop, Elizabeth. **Katharine's Doll.** New York: E.P. Dutton, 1983. 29 pp.

Molly and Katharine are best friends and share many activities until Katharine receives a beautiful new doll. Although Katharine sometimes shares her doll, Molly is very jealous of it. When the two girls start playing exclusively with the doll, they quarrel and declare their friendship is over. Molly and Katharine both grow lonely and decide to pursue other activities together as best friends.

IL: Ages 4-6

7.68 Winthrop. **Tough Eddie.** see Ch. 8.

7.69 Zalben, Jane. "Oh, Simple!" New York: Farrar, Straus, Giroux, 1981. 21 pp.

When Beasely is unable to get his own way at home, he runs away to a friend's house. Beasely's friend has a patronizing attitude and seems to be more skillful than him at just about everything, so Beasely returns home. Beasely is pleased when he discovers the next day that he can do something better than his friend.

IL: Ages 4-6

7.70 Ziefert. **clappity clap!** see Ch. 3.

8

Self-image and Sex Roles

Early-childhood is a critical period for the development of
self-concept. Self-concepts, or images children have of themselves,
are mirror images of what they believe significant people in their
lives--parents, teachers, and peers--think of them(1). If children
believe that significant people think favorably of them, they think
favorably of themselves, and vice versa. The self-concept contains
such elements as meanings related to sex roles, physical self-image,
and psychosocial self-image. It is somewhat difficult to separate these
different aspects of the self-concept from one another as they are all
related and develop in similar ways.

Self-Concept

During the preschool years, children develop certain kinds of
generalized attitudes about themselves--a positive sense of well-being
or a feeling that they are "slow" or naughty. Children also develop a
set of ideals during these years, and as they do, they learn to
measure themselves against what they think they should be. These
early attitudes eventually become basic elements of the individual's
self-concept, but they are often very difficult to explore because
they were partially learned at a nonverbal level(2). A look at the
major theories of development provides differing explanations for how
this happens in the young child.

The process through which children develop a physical and
psychosocial image and learn to identify with a particular sex role has
been explained with three major theories--social learning theory,
psychoanalytic theory, and cognitive-developmental theory. The
process of identification plays a role in all three theories; however,
the processes leading to identification and its importance in each of
the theories vary.

Social learning theory. Social learning theory stresses the child's
imitation of the parents' behavior. If parents perceive themselves in a
positive fashion, then the child will reflect these same positive
feelings of self. Likewise, when the child imitates a parent with low
self-esteem, the result will be a negative self-concept in the child.
What a child may be simply imitating at the age of two becomes an
internalized set of expectations and behavior by age five.

Bandura, a learning theorist, has emphasized the obvious reasons why a child learns to identify with a particular sex role: 1) immediately after birth, a name indicative of sex is often given to a child, 2) the child is many times encouraged to dress in sex-typed clothing and given sex-typed toys to play with, and 3) role-appropriate behaviors from the child are usually reinforced by the parents. The major emphasis of learning theory, then, is that sex-role training starts at birth when appropriate sexual responses are rewarded and sex-inappropriate behaviors are punished(3). Through this process, the child gradually begins to identify with the appropriate gender role.

Psychoanalytic theory. The psychoanalytic point of view stresses the need for a balance of id, ego, and superego forces for an individual to have positive self-feelings. This process starts at birth when the infant is dominated by the id. The primary narcissism, or self-love, of infants prevents them from separating the self from what is nonself. The ego, which is the reality oriented structure, overlaps with and integrates the id forces through rational thought. The development of the superego takes place toward the end of the phallic period, around the age of six. Positive self-esteem is thought by psychoanalysts to involve the interplay of the narcissistic id, the reality oriented ego, and the internalized societal rules of the superego.

Psychoanalytic theorists assume that the parent plays the key role in the child's identification with appropriate sex roles. The process is a complex intrapsychic one that links sexual identification to the resolution of the Oedipus complex for boys and the Electra complex for girls. Each of these complexes creates anxiety in children about their attraction to the parent of the opposite sex. Freud believed that children reduce this anxiety by trying to become more like the parent of the same sex. They actually internalize the attitudes, values, and even the mannerisms of the same sex parent during this process(4).

Cognitive developmental theory. Cognitive developmentalists believe that children's attitudes toward themselves, as well as their knowledge of themselves, result from their increasing cognitive growth and the attitudes of those around them. In the interaction with objects and people at different times in personal growth, various empirical selves are organized. First to develop is an individual's conception of the body, then the sense organs and musculature, and finally the concept of social behavior. During the sensorimotor stage, birth to two years of age, children get an increasingly clearer concept of themselves as individuals separate in body and action from objects and other people. From ages two to seven, the preoperational stage, there is a transition from egocentric to socialized speech; thus the child is able to integrate the self-concept by trying on different roles symbolically and verbalizing self-feelings in relation to others(5). This gradually leads to less egocentricity and the development of a moral structure in the child at six or seven years of age.

The cognitive developmental theory maintains that love and affection for the parents, rather than a resolution of a complex intrapsychic process, bring about sexual identification. It is a child's conception of the body and how it differs from other bodies that determines sexual behavior. This process begins when children are initially labeled "boy" or "girl." These labels become the central organizer and determinant of many of the child's activities, values, and attitudes. Once children have stabilized themselves as to gender, they value positively those objects consistent with this gender and act in accordance with this identity, since there is a need for cognitive consistency.

All three of the developmental theories discussed would agree that the child's self-concept is affected by the family and other sources. Concepts of self are sometimes said to be hierarchical in nature; the **primary** self-concept is acquired first, followed by the **secondary** self-concept.

The **primary** self-concept is founded on the experiences a child has in the home. The strongest influence on a child's developing self-image is the child's parents, since they provide the child with definitions of right and wrong, models of behavior, and the evaluations of actions, on which children base their own ideas(6). In addition to parental teachings and attitudes, a child's self-image is also based on contact with siblings and comparison with siblings.

As contacts outside the home increase, children begin to acquire **secondary** self-concepts. Children who have developed self-concepts characterized by beliefs of their own importance, for example, will select playmates who regard them much as their parents do. Where younger preschool children appear to be most influenced by the home, older preschool children develop an awareness of what peers think of them. Teachers, of course, have a great influence on how children see themselves. Studies concerning the self-fulfilling prophecy conducted by Rosenthal and Jacobson found that children who perceived their teacher's feelings toward them as being favorable saw themselves positively and that teacher expectation has much influence on a child's behavior and school achievement(7).

Generally, though not always, the primary self-concept is more favorable than the secondary. When a discrepancy exists, children must close the gap between the two if they are to be happy and well adjusted. As children move beyond the family, they expect previously rewarded behavior to be approved by significant people in their new social situations. If this does not occur, it is difficult for the child to maintain the old self-image and behavior will most likely change.

Physical and Psychosocial Self-Image

All self-concepts include physical and psychosocial self-images. The physical self-image is usually formed first and is related to the child's physical appearance and the importance of different parts of the body to behavior and to the prestige they give the child in the eyes of others(8). Psychosocial self-images are based on thoughts, feelings, and emotions and consist of abilities that affect adjustment to life such as independence, self-confidence, and so on. Coordinating physical and psychosocial self-images is often difficult for young children. As the child grows older, the physical and psychosocial self-images gradually fuse.

During the preschool years, children first begin to notice that some children are taller than themselves, others are shorter, some are fatter, some thinner, some are stronger, and others are weaker. Although differences in height and weight are not as pronounced at this stage as they are at later stages of development, the extremely tall preschool child and especially the obese preschool child are likely to attract the attention of adults and their peers.

Being able to control their bodies as well as, if not better than, their peers is important to children. One study suggests that activity is the most important factor in the preschool child's self-definition. The children in this study described themselves in terms of such statements as "I can pick up things" and "I wash my hair myself"(9). The learning of dressing and feeding skills gives the preschooler a sense of pride and independence. Parental approval of such skills enhances the child's primary self-concept.

For the older preschool child, being adept at performing certain motor skills brings acceptance from the peer group. Being able to run and skip or learning to ride a bicycle is important to the child as it affects how the child is viewed by peers. Children must view their bodies as being attractive, efficient, and worthwhile for them to see themselves positively and as separate unique individuals.

Where the physical self-image is made up of a child's awareness of physical appearance and motor skills, the psychosocial image takes into account both the psychological and sociological influences affecting the individual. Children as young as three years of age have a basic idea that they have a private self to which others do not have access. At this time, young children distinguish this inner self from their bodily self or outer self. This was evident in an investigation where three-year-olds were asked if an experimenter could see them thinking; for example, one child said the experimenter could not see him thinking because he did not have holes in himself and another child said there was skin over his head which prevented the experimenter from seeing him thinking. After they have developed an understanding that they have a private self, children then set about the task of defining the characteristics of their private selves(10).

Younger preschool children, aged two to four, are highly egocentric—they feel good about themselves and respond to all positive experiences as evidence of their ultimate importance and value. Slightly older children, however, come into contact with adults and peers outside the family. These significant others may not prize their skills or be as understanding about their limitations. Therefore, the older preschool child may experience a temporary decrease in self-esteem. As physical and social competence increases, as thought becomes more flexible, and as the child makes meaningful friendships, the self-esteem should rise again.

In particular, the conquering of most fears and learning to cope with various emotions toward the end of early-childhood enhance the child's psychosocial self-image. It is important for children to accept their flaws and be aware of their strengths as a part of exploring their physical and psychosocial self-images.

Sex Roles

The label "sex role" has been used to describe the different characteristics children display because they are either male or female. However, some experts define sex role as the behaviors that are expected of children because they are either male or female. Children learn appropriate sex-role development through the socialization process. The key social system involved in this learning process is the family. Other systems such as the school, neighborhood, and community also have an important impact on a child's sex-role development.

The changing occupational structure of American society plus the evolving roles of males and females have led to consideration of a theoretical and practical concept called "androgyny." This word comes from two Greek words--andros (male) and gyne (female)--and is often defined as being sex-role flexible(11). The concept of androgyny has emerged as an alternative to traditional sex roles where masculinity and femininity are viewed as opposites. Certain social scientists conclude that sex roles should not be viewed as bipolar sexual extremes, but rather as dualistic dimensions within each other(12). Given the fact that there is more blending of the sex roles between men and women in today's society, an androgynous sex-role orientation within families may contribute to a child's development.

Research by Babladelis appears to support this view. Babladelis found that the classification of a child as androgynous suggested that the child had attributes of masculine and feminine characteristics highly valued by society. Also, the androgynous child was achievement oriented, showed high self-esteem, and was found to be a warm and caring individual(13).

Not everyone agrees with this viewpoint, however. No one argues the existence of genetic, biochemical, and anatomical differences between the sexes. Even environmentally oriented psychologists acknowledge that boys and girls will be treated differently because of their physical differences and their different roles in reproduction(14). Androgyny is certainly not consistent with the psychoanalytic point of view. Regardless of this debate, there are more mothers of young children entering the labor force and more fathers being awarded child custody as the male capacity for nurturing is recognized. Therefore, a child's family orientation largely will affect sex-role identity. A host of social agents outside the family such as teacher expectations and peer relations have an effect on the child's continuing development of a sex role as well.

Self-Image and Sex Roles in
Early Childhood Literature

The preschool child is highly involved in developing a self-concept. Children's books which stress the uniqueness of individuals, both in physical appearance and skills and in thoughts and feelings, provide a vehicle for examination of the self. The development of independence also enhances the child's feelings of self-worth; therefore, books on mastering toilet training and ending such habits as blanket carrying and thumbsucking may be beneficial to the preschooler experiencing such changes.

The development of appropriate sex-role behavior is quite important during the years from two to six. During the last decade, children's literature has reflected changing sex roles. Many children's books now show a father involved in child care while mother is at work, or even a single-parent family headed by a father. Boys are depicted as liking dolls as much as cars and trucks, while girls are portrayed as being more active and adventurous than in past children's literature. In recent years, certain book characters also appear to be androgynous; they have names that are not sex specific and possess facial features and hair styles that are neither masculine nor feminine. Hopefully such characters will convey the message that all children experience the same feelings and have the same needs, regardless of sex. Since sex-role patterns developed during the preschool years have been found to remain remarkably stable throughout adulthood, it appears essential to help children explore literature dealing with this topic.

Responses to the literature. As identification is thought to be the greatest contributer to children developing a positive self-concept and appropriate sex roles, providing positive role models in literature for the purpose of identification would seem to be most important for the preschool child. Discussing occupations mommies can have outside the home and the nurturant feelings daddies can express can help the preschooler explore the changing sex roles evident in today's world. How a child differs from and is similar to certain characters would help individual preschoolers to examine their uniqueness as far as the physical and inner self. The adult guide may want to make use of additional activities such as:
     1) Constructing an **All About Me** book for the child with appropriate illustrations and fill-in statements such as: My name is _____. I am___years old. I weigh___pounds. I like to play_____. I don't like_____. I like to think about_____.
     2) Having dress-up clothes available that depict various occupations, with children role playing their favorite jobs.
     3) Making "Me" buttons or badges with a photograph of the child or a picture of anything that represents the child, stressing the individuality of the badges.
     4) Using a real mirror and a magic mirror made of cellophane, with the child looking in the real mirror and describing the self, then looking in the magic mirror and describing the inner self others don't know about.
     5) Composing a list to accompany the statement: I'm glad I'm me because...(15).

As children learn who and what they are and begin to evaluate themselves as active forces in their worlds, they are putting together a cognitive theory about themselves that helps to integrate their behaviors(16). Children's literature dealing with self-image, whether physical or psychosocial, and books which depict changing sex roles can aid preschool children in exploring their inner and outer selves. The development of a positive self-concept acquired at this point in a child's life can only enhance later stages of development.

NOTES

1. Elizabeth B. Hurlock, **Child Development** 6th ed. (New York: McGraw-Hill, 1978), p. 372.

2. Grace J. Craig, **Human Development** 2d ed. (Englewood Cliffs, New Jersey: Prentice-Hall, 1980), p. 259.

3. P.H. Mussen, "Early Sex Role Development," in **Handbook of Socialization Theory and Research**, edited by D.A. Goslin (Chicago: Rand McNally, 1969).

4. Craig, p. 268.

5. Shirley C. Samuels, **Enhancing Self-Concept in Early Childhood: Theory and Practice** (New York: Human Sciences Press, 1977), p. 32.

6. Craig, p. 260.

7. Robert Rosenthal and Lenor Jacobson, **Pygmalion in the Classroom** (New York: Holt, Rinehart, and Winston, 1968).

8. Hurlock, p. 372.

9. Craig, p. 259.

10. John W. Santrock and Steven R. Yussen, **Children and Adolescents-A Developmental Perspective** (Dubuque, Iowa: William C. Brown, 1984), p. 222.

11. Santrock and Yussen, p. 223.

12. Sandra Bem, "On the Utility of Alternative Procedures for Assessing Psychological Androgyny," **Journal of Consulting and Clinical Psychology** (Volume 45, 1977): 196-205.

13. G. Babladelis, "Accentuate the Positive," **Contemporary Psychology** (Volume 24, 1979): 3-4.

14. Santrock and Yussen, p. 224.

15. Don Dinkmeyer, **Developing Understanding of Self and Others (DUSO) Manual** (Circle Pines, Minnesota: American Guidance Service, 1970); Harry W. Forgan, **The Reading Corner** (Santa Monica: Goodyear Publishing, 1977); Samuels, **Enhancing Self-Concept in Early Childhood.**

16. Craig, p. 260.

BOOKS

8.1 Alda, Arlene. **Sonya's Mommy Works.** New York: Little Simon, 1982. 43 pp.

Five-year old Sonya loves weekends because she doesn't have school and can spend lots of time with her parents. Since her mother has gone back to work, Sonya has made several adjustments--she needs to be more independent with dressing herself and preparing snacks; Sonya has a babysitter who cares for her after school; her father spends more time with her. When Sonya's mother leaves town for several days as part of her job, Sonya is very unhappy. She gets lots of loving attention from her grandmother and father, however, and is glad to welcome her mother back home in time for her birthday.

IL: Ages 4-6

8.2 Andersen, Karen. **What's the Matter, Sylvie, Can't You Ride?** New York: Dial Press, 1981. 26 pp.

Sylvie becomes frustrated and frightened when she tries to learn to ride her new birthday bike. When her friends and even her mother glide by on their bikes, Sylvie angrily kicks her new bike and abandons it. Going back to find it the next day, Sylvie solves her problem when she mistakenly starts down a hill and finds she has to pedal just to stay on.

IL: Ages 4-6

8.3 Asch, Frank. **Goodnight Horsey.** Englewood Cliffs, NJ: Prentice-Hall, 1981. 28 pp.

During her father's nightly ritual of preparing her for bed, a young girl imagines that he turns into a horse. After giving the girl an adventurous ride, the horse slowly turns back into her father who resumes putting his daughter to bed.

IL: Ages 2-4

8.4 Asch, Frank. **Just Like Daddy.** Englewood Cliffs, NJ: Prentice-Hall, 1981. 26 pp.

A very young bear spends his day imitating all the activities his father does. The mother joins them on a fishing trip. Father catches a small fish, but the little bear catches a big fish just like his mother's.

IL: Ages 2-4

8.5 Barbato, Juli. **From Bed to Bus.** New York: Macmillan, 1985. 27 pp.

A young girl has various problems with bathing, brushing her teeth, and dressing each morning as she gets ready for school. With help from her parents and siblings, the girl is able to find a way to overcome each obstacle. She finally becomes an expert at school preparation, if only she could get to her bus stop on time.

IL: Ages 4-6

8.6 Barrett. I'm too small. YOU'RE TOO BIG. see Ch. 6.

8.7 Bauer, Caroline. My Mom Travels a Lot. New York: Frederick Warne, 1981. 32 pp.

Accustomed to her mother's job that requires frequent travelling, a little girl lists the good points and bad points about the situation. Although she greatly misses her mother, the child and her father develop a close relationship and share the household responsibilities. They are both very glad when the mother returns home.

IL: Ages 4-6

8.8 Berenstain, Stan and Jan. The Berenstain Bears and Mama's New Job. New York: Random House, 1984. 29 pp.

When friends and neighbors urge Mama Bear to turn her quilt-making hobby into a business, she rents an empty store much to her family's surprise. Once Mama Bear begins spending time at work, Papa and the two Bear children find they must be more self-reliant and help Mama with the household chores. Although the whole family has some adjustments to make, it is worth it because Mama Bear is so happy.

IL: Ages 4-6

8.9 Brandenberg, Franz. Otto Is Different. New York: Greenwillow Books, 1985. 21 pp.

Otto the octopus laments the fact that he is so different from his friends because of his many arms. His wise parents point out the advantages of having 8 arms--he can get dressed and do his chores 4 times as fast. After a successful hockey game playing goalie, Otto is convinced that being different from others isn't so bad and may prove to be quite advantageous.

IL: Ages 4-6

8.10 Brown. Someone Special, Just Like You. see Ch. 10.

8.11 Caple, Kathy. The Biggest Nose. Boston: Houghton Mifflin, 1985. 32 pp.

Eleanor the elephant becomes quite self-conscious about her large nose when her classmates tease her about it and try to measure it. At home Eleanor twists her nose into a knot in an effort to shorten it. Although her parents and older sister try pulling, using ice, and oiling her nose in attempts to loosen the knot, only Eleanor's sneeze releases the knot. Thankful to have her nose back to normal, Eleanor points out to her classmates the next day that each has different characteristics--biggest mouth, long tail, and so on.

IL: Ages 4-6

8.12 Chevalier, Christa. **Spence Isn't Spence Anymore.** Chicago:
Albert Whitman and Company, 1985. 29 pp.

When Spence declares that he is tired of being Spence, his mother
gives him fuzzy ears and a tail so that he can be Somebody Else.
Somebody Else spends the day doing all the things Spence usually
did, but the next morning Somebody Else is surprised to discover
that mother is wearing a disguise and is now Big Somebody Else.
Spence doesn't like the stranger and Big Somebody Else wishes
Spence would return, so they both remove their disguises to be
mother and son once again.

IL: Ages 4-6

8.13 Cohen, Miriam. **No Good in Art.** New York: Greenwillow Books,
1980. 29 pp.

Convinced that he cannot draw or paint well, Jim watches others in
his class paint a variety of interesting pictures. The art teacher
encourages everyone to be creative and is able to say something
positive about each child's drawing. Finally, Jim begins painting and
he is later pleased when his picture attracts much attention.

IL: Ages 4-6

8.14 Cohen, Miriam. **So What?** New York: Greenwillow Books, 1982. 29
pp.

Jim worries about not performing on the jungle gym, not being the
tallest in his class, and not keeping step during dance class. A
friend advises him that everyone is different, with certain tasks
easier for some children than for others. Although his friend moves
away, Jim conquers the jungle gym and learns to accept himself as he
is.

IL: Ages 4-6

8.15 Cooney, Nancy. **The Blanket that Had to Go.** New York: G.P.
Putnam's Sons, 1981. 27 pp.

Susi is very attached to a tattered old blanket which is her constant
companion. When Susi's mother announces that she cannot take her
blanket to kindergarten, Susi is in despair until she comes up with a
plan. A week before kindergarten begins, Susi's brother cuts her
blanket in half; by the first day of school, it has unravelled until it
is pocket sized.

IL: Ages 4-6

8.16 Davis, Gibbs. **Katy's First Haircut.** Boston: Houghton Mifflin,
1985. 30 pp.

Katy's long hair is always in the way, so she persuades her mother
to take her for a haircut. Once her hair is cut, however, Katy wants

to put it back and wears a hat to school. Katy eventually finds that there are real advantages to having short hair and she reassures a friend about to get a haircut.

IL: Ages 4-6

8.17 Davis, Gibbs. **The Other Emily.** Boston: Houghton Mifflin, 1984. 32 pp.

Young Emily writes her name everywhere and possesses a nightlight and T-shirt bearing her name. Therefore, she is surprised and later outraged on her first day of school when she discovers that there is another Emily in her class. Her parents are sympathetic when Emily claims she is no longer special. When both Emilys bring the same item for Show 'n Tell the following day, they agree to participate together and consider being friends.

IL: Ages 4-6

8.18 Delton, Judy. **I Never Win!** Minneapolis: Carolrhoda Books, 1981. 32 pp.

After repeatedly losing races and games to his peers, Charlie becomes quite discouraged. To ease his anger at not winning, he practices the piano for hours at a time. When Charlie's piano teacher requests that he play for her guests and he is applauded loudly, Charlie feels he has finally won at something.

IL: Ages 4-6

8.19 Dickinson. **My Brother's Silly.** see Ch. 4.

8.20 Elliot. **Two Wheels for Grover.** see Ch. 6.

8.21 Fitzhugh. **I Am Four.** see Ch. 6.

8.22 Fitzhugh. **I Am Three.** see Ch. 6.

8.23 Frankel, Alona. **Once Upon a Potty.** Woodbury, NY: Barron's Educational Service, 1980. 32 pp.

A little boy, Joshua, and his mother are introduced, whereupon she describes the functions of various body parts. Expressing her weariness at diaper changing, Joshua's mother is pleased when he receives a potty. Joshua explores various uses for the potty, but discovers its main purpose is for elimination. It is stressed that potty training is a slow process and although Joshua continues to have accidents, he and his mother are overjoyed when he finally has success on the potty.

IL: Ages 2-4

8.24 Galloway, Priscilla. **When You Were Little and I Was Big.** Toronto: Annick Press, 1984. 28 pp.

A little girl imagines that she is the adult and her mother, a child.

As an adult, the little girl describes what she would do: never get mad when the child woke up early, take the child to work, play and pretend with the child, always read one extra story at night, etc. In short, the little girl describes herself as a good parent, just like her own mother.

IL: Ages 2-6

8.25 Greenberg, Polly. **I Know I'm Myself Because...** New York: Human Sciences Press, 1981. 25 pp.

Through observations about herself, a young girl begins to discover her self-identity. She shows an awareness of her growing body, of the range of emotions she feels, and of her physical abilities. By exploring how she is like other children and how she is different, the child realizes her uniqueness within her family and in school.

IL: Ages 4-6

8.26 Henkes. **All Alone.** see Ch. 2.

8.27 Henkes, Kevin. **Clean Enough.** New York: Greenwillow Books, 1982. 21 pp.

As he soaks in the bathtub, a young boy remembers when his father used to bathe him and decides he must be growing bigger because the tub seems smaller. Now he's too busy playing and pretending to take time to wash himself. He assumes he is clean enough when his mother calls for him to get out of the tub.

IL: Ages 4-6

8.28 Hines, Anna. **All By Myself.** Boston: Houghton Mifflin, 1985. 28 pp.

Declaring that she hates wearing a nighttime diaper, Josie convinces her mother to let her sleep without one. Sure enough Josie wakes up that night and her mother helps her use the bathroom. One night she sleeps through and has a wet bed, followed by a night of Josie waking up time and again to use the bathroom. Her mother is so weary the next night that Josie can't arouse her, so she bravely turns on the light and heads for the bathroom all by herself.

IL: Ages 2-4

8.29 Hoban. **No, No, Sammy Crow.** see Ch. 4.

8.30 Horner. **Little Big Girl.** see Ch. 6.

8.31 Jonas. **When You Were a Baby.** see Ch. 6.

8.32 Keller. **Cromwell's Glasses.** see Ch. 10.

8.33 Keller, Holly. **Geraldine's Blanket.** New York: Greenwillow Books, 1984. 28 pp.

Very attached to her baby blanket, Geraldine the pig takes it everywhere and helps wash and mend it. When Geraldine's parents decide she is too old to carry around a blanket, they unsuccessfully try to hide it and then try to replace the blanket with a new doll. Still adamant about wanting her blanket near her, Geraldine solves the problem by making clothes for her new doll out of the blanket.

IL: Ages 2-6

8.34 Kempler, Susan, Doreen Rappaport, and Michele Spirn. **A Man Can Be...** New York: Human Sciences Press, 1981. 27 pp.

A father and his young son spend the day together with such activities as preparing a meal, visiting a playground, and getting ready for bed illustrated. A man's ability to express many emotions ranging from anger to nurturing is stressed. The boy's father is seen as a friend, as well as a caring adult and role model for the child.

IL: Ages 4-6

8.35 Levenson, Kathe. **When I Grow Up and You Grow Down.** New York: Lothrop, Lee, and Shepard, 1983. 29 pp.

A child imagines all the benefits if she were to switch roles with her mother: she could go out for the evening and get a babysitter for her mother, she could order her mother to clean her bedroom, she could eat sweets and snacks while her mother ate nutritious food. However, when the little girl considers having no one to tuck her into bed, brush her hair, or comfort her when she's hurt, she decides that perhaps it's best to remain a child for a while.

IL: Ages 4-6

8.36 Lloyd. **Nandy's Bedtime.** see Ch. 4.

8.37 Long, Earlene. **Gone Fishing.** Boston: Houghton Mifflin, 1984. 32 pp.

In preparation for a fishing trip, daddy has a big breakfast and gets his big fishing rod while his young son eats a little breakfast and finds his little fishing rod. The two spend the day together fishing and eating lunch; they are surprised when the little boy catches a big fish as well as a small one and daddy catches one of each size too.

IL: Ages 2-4

8.38 McDaniel. **Katie Couldn't.** see Ch. 6.

8.39 McPhail, David. **Pig Pig Grows Up.** New York: E.P. Dutton, 1980. 22 pp.

As the youngest of his family, Pig Pig refuses to grow up. He eats baby food, wears baby clothes, throws tantrums, and sleeps in a crib. His parents finally give up on encouraging him to grow up. However, when Pig Pig is faced with an emergency, he decides to grow up very quickly and is a hero afterwards.

IL: Ages 2-6

8.40 Mitchell, Joyce. **My Mommy Makes Money.** Boston: Little, Brown, and Company, 1984. 31 pp.

Mothers are shown with various occupations, including many jobs which are traditionally male-oriented such as carpenter, appliance repairer, surgeon, and minister. Certain children visit their mothers at work, while all show pride in their mothers' accomplishments.

IL: Ages 4-6

8.41 Moncure. NOW I AM FIVE! see Ch. 6.

8.42 Moncure. NOW I AM FOUR! see Ch. 6.

8.43 Moncure. NOW I AM THREE! see Ch. 6.

8.44 Moncure. NOW I AM TWO! see Ch. 6.

8.45 Newman, Alyse. **It's Me, Claudia!** New York: Franklin Watts, 1981.   28 pp.

Unhappy with the size of her ears, Claudia unsuccessfully tries to tape and paste them down. She is pleased when she discovers that her mother's hat will hide her ears; however, the hat covers most of her face as well causing Claudia to become accident prone. When friends don't recognize her with the hat on, Claudia decides to remove it and accept her appearance.

IL: Ages 4-6

8.46 Ormerod, Jan. **Dad's Back.** New York: Lothrop, Lee, and Shepard, 1985. 16 pp.

A baby delights in father's return and explores what dad has brought back with him. Then the two play chase, tickling, etc.

IL: Ages 2-4

8.47 Parish, Peggy. **I Can—Can You? (Levels 1, 2, 3, 4)** New York: Greenwillow Books, 1980. 10 pp. each.

A series of progressively more difficult physical and social skills are presented. Toddlers are illustrated in Level 1 waving good-bye, playing peek-a-boo, and so on. Level 2 focuses on such activities as block play and mastering eating and drinking skills, while bathroom skills, running, and jumping are mentioned in Level 3. Sharing, saying please and thank you, bathing, and dressing are all demonstrated by preschoolers in Level 4.

IL: Ages 2-6

8.48 Pomerantz, Charlotte. **Posy.** New York: Greenwillow Books, 1983. 48 pp.

Posy and her father spend quality time together with him telling her stories about when she was a toddler. The stories stress her parents' warmth and caring attitude, with respect shown for Posy's decisions as a child. The good father-daughter relationship still exists as the father finishes reminiscing and tucks Posy into bed.

IL: Ages 4-6

8.49 Rabe. **The Balancing Girl.** see Ch. 10.

8.50 Robison, Deborah. **Bye-Bye, Old Buddy.** New York: Clarion Books, 1983. 28 pp.

Although she still loves her old baby blanket, Jenny comes to the conclusion that she has outgrown the need for it. Jenny considers burying her old blanket, raffling it off, or attaching balloons to it and letting it float away. Finally Jenny mails her blanket to a random address picked from the phone book, hoping that person will appreciate it. Sure enough, unknown to Jenny, her blanket is used by an old man for his puppies' bed.

IL: Ages 4-6

8.51 Rockwell. **Can I Help?** see Ch. 4.

8.52 Rockwell, Anne. **When We Grow Up.** New York: E.P. Dutton, 1981. 29 pp.

Children are illustrated in the occupations they want to have when they grow up. Along with traditional sex-role occupations, men as teachers and artists as well as women who are astronauts, plumbers and mechanics are depicted.

IL: Ages 4-6

8.53 Rosenberg. **My Friend Leslie...** see Ch. 10.

8.54 Schwartz, Amy. **Bea and Mr. Jones.** Scarsdale, NY: Bradbury Press, 1982. 29 pp.

Tired of kindergarten activities, Bea agrees to trade places with her executive father for one day. Bea loves the hectic pace of her father's advertising job and her father excels in his kindergarten subjects. Both are so happy with their new roles, they decide to make the arrangement permanent.

IL: Ages 4-6

8.55 Simon, Norma. **Nobody's Perfect, Not Even My Mother.** Chicago: Albert Whitman and Company, 1981. 28 pp.

Several children realize that no one is perfect, not even the adults in their lives--parents, teachers, and grandparents. However, just as each of the adults has an area he or she excels in, so do the children. Although each child makes mistakes, each has a special achievement to be proud of.

IL: Ages 4-6

8.56 Stanovich. **Big Boy, Little Boy.** see Ch. 6.

8.57 Stecher, Miriam and Alice Kandell. **Daddy and Ben Together.** New York: Lothrop, Lee, and Shepard, 1981. 24 pp.

Ben and his father share many activities, yet they find it difficult to adjust to Ben's mother being away from home with her new job. Ben pouts because his father runs the household differently and always seems to be tired. After the two have a picnic and spend the day playing together, they anticipate Ben's mother's return while discovering they can make it on their own.

IL: Ages 4-6

8.58 Szekeres. **Puppy Too Small.** see Ch. 6.

8.59 Szekeres, Cyndy. **Thumpity Thump Gets Dressed.** Racine, WI: Western Publishing, 1984. 19 pp.

Thumpity Thump the rabbit exhibits his prowess at dressing when he dons a variety of clothing and outer garments during the course of a day. It seems that each time he dresses to go outside, the weather changes and he needs to put on different clothing. Finally Papa helps Thumpity into his pajamas and the little rabbit claims he can dream about dressing for any type of weather he wishes.

IL: Ages 2-4

8.60 Thomson and Beck. **My Bear: I Can...Can You?** see Ch. 6.

8.61 Titherington, Jeanne. **Big World, Small World.** New York: Greenwillow Books, 1985. 21 pp.

On Saturday Anna and her mother spend the day together, yet their experiences are not always the same because of their difference in size, etc. Mother looks at her face in the mirror, while Anna checks her toes. Anna drinks milk and her mother gets coffee for breakfast. Mother takes her purse to the store and looks for items they need; Anna takes her teddy bear and looks for things she wants. However, at the end of the day they both give Anna's father a hug and kiss.

IL: Ages 4-6

8.62 Tusa. **Libby's New Glasses.** see Ch. 10.

8.63 von Konigslow, Andrea. **Toilet Tales.** Toronto: Annick Press, 1985. 22 pp.

Explanations are given for why different kinds of animals could never use a toilet--a giraffe couldn't fit through the door, an elephant would smash it, a seal would slip off, etc. A toilet is therefore described as appropriate only for big boys and big girls.

IL: Ages 2-4

8.64 Walsh, Ellen. **Theodore All Grown** Up. Garden City, NY: Doubleday and Company, 1981. 27 pp.

When Theodore decides he has become a grown-up overnight, he thinks about all the adult privileges he will now have. After his parents advise Theodore to give away all of his toys, Theodore sorts through his toy box and discovers he does not feel ready to give away some of his most prized possessions. He does find a few baby toys he has outgrown, however, and decides although he's not a grown-up yet, he has grown up a little bit.

IL: Ages 4-6

8.65 Wandro, Mark and Joani Blank. **My Daddy is a Nurse.** Reading, MA: Addison-Wesley, 1981. 29 pp.

Daddies with traditional jobs are mentioned, but the focus is on daddies with occupations usually associated with women. Along with a description of their work, daddies are illustrated who are flight attendants, preschool teachers, librarians, ballet dancers, etc. The book concludes with a daddy who is a homemaker busy caring for house and children.

IL: Ages 4-6

8.66 Watanabe, Shigeo. **Daddy, play with me!** New York: G.P. Putnam's Sons, 1984. 28 pp.

A young bear and his father become quite involved in playing. Father and son seem to equally enjoy dancing, sharing a piggyback ride, playing horse, and becoming a train and airplane together. After father reads a story, both are tired enough to take a nap.

IL: Ages 2-4

8.67 Watanabe. **Get set! Go!** see Ch. 6.

8.68 Watanabe, Shigeo. **How do I put it on?** New York: G.P. Putnam's Sons, 1980. 28 pp.

Although he has difficulties with each piece of clothing, a small bear demonstrates that he is able to dress himself with no help.

IL: Ages 2-4

8.69 Watanabe. **I can ride it.** see Ch. 6.

8.70 Watanabe. **I'm the king of the castle.** see Ch. 5.

8.71 Watson. **Jamie's Story.** see Ch. 4.

8.72 Weiss, Nicki. **Hank and Oogie.** New York: Greenwillow Books, 1982. 29 pp.

As a baby Hank receives a stuffed hippo, Oogie, and the two become inseparable friends for the next few years. Although Hank is too embarrassed to take Oogie to kindergarten, at home he still eats with, bathes with, and goes to bed with his stuffed animal. When Oogie needs to be laundered and allowed to dry, Hank must perform his daily routine without Oogie. Finding he is able to go it alone, Hank places Oogie on a shelf with other toys he has outgrown.

IL: Ages 4-6

8.73 Winthrop, Elizabeth. **Tough Eddie.** New York: E.P. Dutton, 1985. 28 pp.

Eddie likes to play cowboys to feel tough, so he is embarrassed when his older sister tells his friends about the dollhouse in his closet. At nursery school the next day, Eddie avoids his friends. When Eddie stands still until a bee flies off of him, however, everyone in his class admires his bravery. Feeling more secure now, Eddie even considers bringing his dollhouse to show at school the next day.

IL: Ages 4-6

8.74 Ziefert, Harriet. **zippety zip!** New York: Viking Press, 1984. 14 pp.

A young boy takes pride in being able to dress himself, brush his teeth, wash his face, etc.

IL: Ages 2-4

9

Single-parent and Blended Families

An increasing number of families is in transition mainly due to the growing divorce rate. The proportion of children living in intact families has decreased from 79 percent in 1960 to 65 percent in 1982. This has resulted in more and more children living in single-parent families, approximately 22 percent(1). If the present trend continues, a child born today has roughly a 49 percent chance of living in a single-parent family system for some period of time and this experience is not likely to be brief(2). Even though the number of blended families has not significantly increased over the past decade, approximately 1 in 10 children live in this kind of family system(3). The blended family is a family reconstituted from other family systems that have broken up.

The transition of the family has created a number of problems for children involved in this process. It should be realized that many children entering single-parent or blended family systems have experienced the divorce of their biological parents. Divorce as a process is difficult for most children(4). Memories of the past family system may impact the child's adjustment in the single-parent or blended family system. A number of other conflicts are also likely to be present in the child, many related to the child's age. Clearly children living with single parents or in blended families have a number of unique issues to deal with that are significantly different from those of children in intact families.

Single Parents

In order to understand the issues confronting children in single-parent family systems, one must look closely at the nature of these systems. One striking feature is that most single-parent families are headed by women, approximately 90 percent. Even though more fathers are being awarded custody of their children, this practice continues to be the exception to the rule.

The tradition of awarding custody of the child to the mother is based in part on the sweeping impact of psychoanalytic theory at the turn of the twentieth century(5). Traditionally, psychoanalytic approaches stress that mothers are uniquely suited to care for the young. Judges consequently have been likely to award custody of children to their mothers because it is assumed to be in the best interest of the child, unless the mother is judged to be emotionally unstable or severely handicapped in some other way(6).

There is currently a growing trend to award custody of children on the basis of the actual needs of the child. This involves a careful screening of the psychological climate in which the child would live. As the court systems use this approach more and more in the future, it will likely result in greater numbers of fathers being given custody of their children. In a sense, this would appear to be a positive trend. First, the child's needs are considered to be the basis of awarding custody. Secondly, many fathers who are very capable of parenting will now get custody whereas in the past this was extremely unlikely.

Even with the ongoing debate over the role of mothers and fathers as single parents, several important issues need to be pointed out in regard to single-parent families. One of the most striking social problems confronting the single-parent family is poverty(7). A large percentage of these families is below the poverty level. Another important concern is the overburdening role responsibility of the single parent. The single parent must play multiple roles due to the absent spouse. Children in single-parent families may also have to assume increased responsibility at home because of the absent parent. Children in intact families are not necessarily confronted with this issue.

Blended Families

Most people who divorce remarry. This means that children in these families will likely sooner or later end up in a blended family system. The role of parents in blended families has always been difficult in Western society(8). Examples of this difficulty would be a mother finding herself rearing children from her husband's first marriage, children from her first marriage, as well as children from the blended family system. Obviously, role conflicts and problems with loyalty would be pronounced in this kind of arrangement. Through the eyes of a child, the conflict probably seems even greater.

The factors that complicate the roles in blended families are as follows:
1) Parents in blended families do not start at birth; they follow a preceding father or mother. If the child's relationship with the first parent was positive, this creates problems for the new parent in the blended family.
2) Parents in blended families have a tendency to push the new relationships within the blended family too fast or too hard.
3) The complex sets of children in the blended family make discipline at times problematic. It is difficult for parents not to treat their biological children differently from other children in the family.
4) Parents in blended families at times attempt to replace a child's former parent. This is an almost impossible role to play(9).

For all of the above reasons and more, parenting in blended families is a difficult task. This does not mean that there are not positive aspects of blended families. Anne Simon has written extensively on this subject(10). One point she makes, for example, is that literally millions of children would not have a father or mother in the home if it were not for blended families.

Clearly a sizeable number of families and children operate under less than ideal conditions. Regardless of whether a family is a single-parent system, a blended system, or an intact system, all have unique problems that affect the development of children.

Preschool Children And Families In Transition

The two- to six-year-old in the single-parent or blended family system obviously will be confronted with issues much different than children at other stages of development. It is very difficult for the preschool child, for example, to understand why one parent is no longer present or why the child must have a new parent. Children in the preschool stage may blame themselves for the loss of a parent and may even experience mourning because of the now absent parent. The older child responds much differently to the changes resulting from the break-up of the family.

In a study of the effects of parental divorce conducted by Wallerstein and Kelly, the very young preschool child often exhibited regression, confusion, sadness, and fear during the first year after the parental break-up. The older preschool child, five to six years of age, usually showed heightened anxiety and aggressiveness when the parents separated. However, the older group, unlike the younger ones, seemed to have a reasonable understanding of divorce-related changes in the family(11).

Another important concern is possible changes in the single parent's attitude toward parenting. During the first year after break-up, Wallerstein and Kelly found that twice as many parents changed their parenting attitudes as remained the same. This means that many formerly anxious, rejecting parents became closer to their children; however, previously affectionate parents often became more estranged and neglectful as well(12). In either case, during the first year after parental separation, the preschool child often must cope with a different parenting style. As discussed in the chapter on Family Relationships, Baumrind has categorized three major types of parent-child interaction which have a definite impact on a child's development(13). Between the ages of two and six, the child is involved in many developmental changes ranging from expression of emotions to absorbing a value base which make parenting difficult for the two-parent family; the single parent of a preschool child has even more to cope with in the way of parenting.

When a preschool child enters a blended family system, the interaction between the child and the new parent is impacted by a number of factors. Interaction may be strained by the preschooler's memories of the absent parent. If the child does not know the new parent well prior to the constitution of the blended family, adjustment will probably take longer for both the child and the new parent. Again, if the new parent's child-rearing methods differ radically from those of the absent biological parent, the preschool child must try to adjust to this new parenting interaction and conflict may occur. If the child has little affection for the new parent and shows it, problems are likely to arise(14).

As is true in the intact family, the preschooler in a blended family may have problems with sibling relations. The jealousy and rivalry which exist between all siblings may be heightened between stepsiblings. Just as it is important for any siblings to have their own physical space, stepsiblings within the blended family have this need in particular. The arrival of a new sibling is always a traumatic time for older children; within a blended family where the preschooler may be having problems fitting in anyway, a new baby may be cause for great anxiety.

The preschool child in any type of family system has basically the same needs for positive development. The child needs to know what to expect from parents in terms of parenting style. The preschooler needs much nurturing and support from one or more parental figures, whether the child is part of a two-parent home, a single-parent household, or a blended family system. As far as any type of sibling relations, the preschooler needs to be considered as a unique individual with adequate parental time alone.

Single-Parent and Blended Families
in Early Childhood Literature

There are portrayals in children's literature of families growing together, in close, undisrupted units. There are also some portrayals, although not many, of parents who grow apart and whose divergent ways eventually result in divorce(15). Considering the dramatic increase in divorce statistics, there is a need for many more picture books for the preschooler depicting the single-parent family and the blended family. Although there has been a vast increase in literature concerning families in transition for the middle school aged child and the adolescent, there is still a need for more books in this area for the preschooler. Those few early-childhood books which are available deal with the unique stresses inherent in these family systems and depict characters who are able to manage within their new family situation. Certain characters even become aware of advantages they possess because of the family systems they are a part of.

As with any picture books dealing with family relationships, the character in the single-parent or blended family household must establish positive interaction with parents as a foundation for expanding relationships with peers, teachers, and others outside the home. Household routines and responsibilities expected of children are mentioned in most of the books. Difficulties in sharing possessions and parental time with siblings are a particular issue in books concerning blended families. In short, children's literature dealing with families in transition explores the same elements of family relationships dealt with in books about intact families, only with a different family arrangement evident.

Responses to the literature. Picture books about single-parent homes and blended families provide an excellent opportunity for a child in one of these family systems to explore feelings. Many of the very realistic characters appear to be quite easy for the preschool child to identify with. Follow-up activities for these books resemble those used after the reading of any book on family relationships. The helping individual can encourage responses from the child who is part of a family in transition by:

1) Having the child make a collage from magazine pictures depicting various family types--single-parent, one with many children, one which includes a grandparent in the home, etc.

2) Developing a child's weekly schedule, including time spent with a non-custody parent.

3) Constructing the child's family tree, using actual photographs of family members if possible.

4) Writing a short letter dictated by the child to a book character that is admired.

5) Drawing pictures in sequence or making a TV scroll of important incidents in a story which the child may have also experienced(16).

With the increasing number of children who currently reside in a single-parent or blended family, there is an obvious need for an abundance of children's literature concerning this issue for all age groups, including preschoolers. In picture books the family is most frequently drawn as a warm, safe haven where the young child is offered love and understanding; it is essential that children's literature portraying the single-parent and blended family reflect this security as well. The family in any form is essential for optimum physical, social, and emotional development in the child aged two to six.

NOTES

1. **United States Bureau of the Census** (Washington, D.C.: United States Printing Office, 1983).

2. **United States Bureau of the Census.**

3. **United States Bureau of the Census.**

4. Julius Segal and Herbert Yahraes, **A Child's Journey** (New York: McGraw-Hill, 1979), pp. 160-170.

5. John W. Santrock and Steven R. Yussen, **Children and Adolescents-A Developmental Perspective** (Dubuque, Iowa: William C. Brown, 1984), p. 287.

6. Santrock and Yussen, p. 287.

7. Theodore J. Stein, **Social Work Practice in Child Welfare** (Englewood Cliffs, New Jersey: Prentice-Hall, 1981), p. 12.

8. E.E. LeMaster, **Parents in Modern America** 3d ed. (Homewood, Illinois: The Dorsey Press, 1977), p. 146.

9. LeMaster, p. 148.

10. Anne Simon, **Stepchild in the Family** (New York: Odyssey Press, 1964).

11. Judith S. Wallerstein and Joan B. Kelly, "The Effects of Parental Divorce: Experiences of the Preschool Child," **Journal of Child Psychiatry** (Volume 14, No. 4, 1975): 600-616.

12. Wallerstein and Kelly.

13. Diana Baumrind, "Current Patterns of Parental Authority," **Developmental Psychology Monographs** (Volume IV, 1971): 1.

14. Elizabeth B. Hurlock, **Child Development** 6th ed. (New York: McGraw-Hill, 1978), p. 508.

15. Myra Sadker and David Sadker, **Now Upon a Time: A Contemporary View of Children's Literature** (New York: Harper and Row, 1977), p. 29.

16. Jean A. Pardeck and John T. Pardeck, **Young People with Problems: A Guide to Bibliotherapy** (Westport, Connecticut: Greenwood Press, 1984); Shirley C. Samuels, **Enhancing Self-Concept in Early Childhood – Theory and Practice** (New York: Human Sciences Press, 1977); Ellen Weiss, **Sesame Street – My Memory Book** (New York: Children's Television Workshop, 1983).

BOOKS

9.1 Boegehold, Betty. **Dad Doesn't Live Here Anymore.** Racine, WI: Western Publishing, 1985. 23 pp.

Young Casey is accustomed to much quarreling between her parents, yet she is surprised when her dad leaves their home. The first night with her father gone is especially difficult for Casey. The following day she pretends to be sick so that her father comes by her house to check on her, then she decides to run away. Instead Casey acts out her family's problems with her dolls and realizes that she will still get to see her father, just not as often.

IL: Ages 4-6

9.2 Delton, Judy. **My Mother Lost Her Job Today.** Chicago: Albert Whitman, 1980. 29 pp.

A little girl worries that nothing will ever be the same when her mother announces that she has lost her job. That night as she attempts to fall asleep, the child even considers seeking employment herself. Although her mother admits she is angry and tearful right now, she reassures her daughter that eventually she will find another job and things will be OK.

IL: Ages 4-6

9.3 Dragonwagon, Crescent. **Always, Always.** New York: Macmillan, 1984. 26 pp.

Feeling sad yet excited, a little girl is driven to the airport by her mother to go visit her father's home. She thinks about the activities she and her dad will share during the summer, as well as how much she will miss her mother. The little girl's mother reassures her that although her parents divorced because of their differences, they both agree on how much they love her.

IL: Ages 4-6

9.4 Drescher, Joan. **Your Family, My Family.** New York: Walker and Company, 1980. 32 pp.

Various family forms are described—a two-parent family where both parents work, an adopted child's family, a family where child custody is shared, two children in a foster family, etc. Stressed are the strengths of family life such as the sense of belonging, sharing with others, and working together.

IL: Ages 4-6

9.5 Jong, Erica. **Megan's Book of Divorce.** New York: New American Library, 1984. 58 pp.

Four year old Megan describes some of the inconveniences of having divorced parents—having two kitchens to become familiar with,

misplacing clothes and toys, and so on. She describes life before her
parents separated. Both her mom and dad have "friends" who try to
win Megan over, but she fantasizes about their demise and her
parents getting back together. After a big family brunch, Megan
realizes there may be some advantages to divorce--a pet at each
house and twice as many birthday presents.

IL: Ages 4-6

9.6 Jukes, Mavis. **Like Jake and Me**. New York: Alfred A. Knopf,
1984. 28 pp.

Alex is in awe of his strong, brave stepfather, but sometimes feels
he may get in his stepfather's way. He is also unsure of his feelings
about his mother being pregnant. Alex discovers that Jake has a fear
of spiders when one is crawling on him. He is able to rid his
stepfather of the spider, forming a bond between the two.

IL: Ages 4-6

9.7 Keats, Ezra. **Louie's Search**. New York: Scholastic, 1980. 28 pp.

When Louie searches the neighborhood for a new father, the junk man
accuses Louie of stealing something and chases him back home.
Louie's mother reassures the junk man that her son would never steal
and invites him in for tea. The junk man then starts regularly
visiting Louie's home. Louie gets a new father when the junk man
and his mother decide to marry.

IL: Ages 4-6

9.8 Lindsay, Jeanne. **Do I Have a Daddy?** Buena Park, CA: Morning
Glory Press, 1982. 44 pp.

After playing with a friend from a two-parent home, Erik runs home
to ask his single mother whether he has a daddy. Erik's mother tries
to explain--he does have a father whom she loved at one time; his
father saw Erik as a baby; his father left because he was unable to
accept responsibility for a baby. When Erik seems a little sad, his
mother suggests that he spend more time with his uncle and
grandfather. Included are suggestions for single parents answering
their children's questions; the importance of honesty, using positive
points, and examining feelings are all stressed.

IL: Ages 2-6

9.9 Noble, June. **Where Do I Fit In?** New York: Holt, Rinehart, and
Winston, 1981. 29 pp.

When John's mother and new stepfather plan a visit to the zoo, John
is too upset to go because his mother is expecting a baby. John is
unsure of his own place within the new family until he spends the
day with his stepfather's parents. There he is assured that his new
grandparents feel he is a very important member of the family and
that the baby will not take John's place.

IL: Ages 4-6

9.10 Seuling, Barbara. **What Kind of Family is This?** Racine, WI: Western Publishing, 1985. 23 pp.

When Jeff's mother gets remarried, he finds himself moving into a house with an all new family. Jeff still loves his father and doesn't really want another dad. He also hates sharing with his new stepsiblings. Jeff and his stepbrother even divide their bedroom in half, but later decide to fix up the room together. Jeff finds it just takes time to get used to his new family situation.

IL: Ages 4-6

9.11 Sharmat. **Sometimes Mama and Papa Fight.** see Ch. 4.

9.12 Shyer, Marlene. **Stepdog.** New York: Charles Scribner's Sons, 1983. 27 pp.

When his father decides to remarry, Terry is happy to make his fun-loving stepmother part of their family. However, his stepmother's dog is jealous of all the attention Terry is getting and starts making life miserable for the rest of them. After the stepdog is banished from the house, Terry begins to empathize with the dog's problems and the two become friends.

IL: Ages 4-6

9.13 Stinson, Kathy. **Mom and Dad Don't Live Together Any More.** Toronto: Annick Press, 1984. 23 pp.

A little girl lives with her mother in the city and spends weekends in the country with her father. She wonders about the reasons her parents separated and sometimes wishes they would get back together, though they have assured her they won't. She thinks about fun things she does with each of her parents and realizes they both love her very much.

IL: Ages 4-6

9.14 Strathdee, Jean. **The House that Grew.** New York: Oxford University Press, 1980. 31 pp.

Rachel, her mother, and their friend Nick live in a big house that they share with several other people. When Nick and her mother decide to move to the country and build a small house, Rachel is delighted with their new life. As winter approaches, the little house seems too crowded so to make all of them more comfortable, a play house is built for Rachel's possessions.

IL: Ages 4-6

9.15 Tax, Meredith. **Families.** Boston: Little, Brown, and Company, 1981. 32 pp.

Six year old Angie lives with her mother most of the time, but spends vacations with her father, her stepmother, and their new baby. Angie describes the family forms of various children she knows--an extended family, a two-parent family, a child who's adopted, a single father home, etc. Angie claims the important thing in all families is how much they love each other.

IL: Ages 4-6

9.16 Van Woerkom, Dorothy. **Something to Crow About.** Chicago: Albert Whitman, 1982. 29 pp.

When Ralph the rooster discovers a basketful of orphaned eggs on his porch, he decides to keep them and hatch them himself. Ralph's friend Harriet the hen gives him much support during the hatching process and offers helpful advice on feeding and caring for newborn chicks. As the chicks grow up, Ralph becomes quite capable of single parenthood and continues to share his joys and concerns with Harriet.

IL: Ages 4-6

9.17 Vigna, Judith. **Daddy's New Baby.** Chicago: Albert Whitman, 1982. 29 pp.

A young girl with divorced parents resents her father's and stepmother's new baby. When she visits her father, the girl has to share a room with the baby and share her father's attention as well. She helps her father prepare the baby for an outing and saves the baby from a near disaster. Discovering that only she can make the baby stop crying, the little girl becomes more fond of her stepsister.

IL: Ages 4-6

9.18 Vigna, Judith. **Grandma Without Me.** Chicago: Albert Whitman, 1984. 29 pp.

A young boy with newly divorced parents longs to spend Thanksgiving with his paternal grandmother as he always has. However, his father and new stepmother will be at grandmother's for the holidays and the little boy's mother says things are different now. The child remembers good times with his grandmother and prepares something special to send her. His mother assures him that next year they will both once again be at grandmother's table for Thanksgiving.

IL: Ages 4-6

9.19 Vigna, Judith. **She's Not My Real Mother.** Chicago: Albert Whitman, 1980. 30 pp.

While spending a weekend with his father and stepmother, Miles is determined to not like his new stepmother no matter how hard she tries to be friendly. His father has work to do on Sunday, so Miles must accompany his stepmother to an ice show. There he purposely gets lost to worry his stepmother. Once she finds Miles, his stepmother says she will not tell his father about the incident and Miles decides to become her friend.

IL: Ages 4-6

9.20 Waber, Bernard. **Bernard.** Boston: Houghton Mifflin, 1982. 48 pp.

After his owners have a quarrel and decide to break up, Bernard the dog cannot decide which one to live with. Bernard runs away instead and wanders the streets trying to attract the attention of someone wanting a new dog. During a rainstorm, Bernard's owners find him and make arrangements to share his care.

IL: Ages 4-6

10

Special Developmental Needs

No two people are exactly alike and individual differences are clearly universal. Weight, height, and physique among human beings often vary greatly. These extreme differences found among people make it difficult to define what we mean by "normality." We typically define "normal" as being average, ordinary, or commonplace, while "abnormal" is viewed as things we do not understand or that are unusual. Unfortunately, those children labeled as having special needs may be viewed as falling outside the "normal" range. This label can often become a greater problem for the child than the actual special need itself. Buscaglia expresses this view as follows:

"Though they may not be aware of it at the time, the infant born with a birth defect and the adult who is crippled later in life, will be limited not so much by the actual disability as much as by society's attitude regarding the disability. It is society, for the most part, that will define the disability as a handicap and it is the individual who will suffer from this definition"(1).

The ways in which a child reacts to a special need will influence the child's development. Some children will try to compensate for their special need by achieving success in an area not affected by their special condition. Other children with a special need will develop a feeling of inadequacy and inferiority due to the special need; for example, a child who needs to wear a leg brace often feels self-conscious, as does a child needing to wear something as commonplace as eyeglasses. The sensitive helping person is aware of these reactions in children and realizes the consequences they may have on the child's development.

Special Needs In
Preschool Children

Children with special needs may become quite evident during the preschool years, as compared to infancy. A child who is deaf or hearing-impaired is particularly disadvantaged because these special needs impact language development. Although the child's concept formation may not necessarily be limited, prelingual deafness makes it difficult for children to communicate with others, use verbal mediation for problem-solving, gain information through hearing, and understand abstract ideas which are most easily explained in linguistic terms(2).

During the early-childhood years, deaf children may appear conceptually limited because of problems in language development. Visually and physically handicapped children often develop language normally, but lack of sensory perception and mobility may seriously limit conceptual formation. Two other special needs not stressed in this chapter, preschoolers with mental disabilities and those with emotional problems, are associated with a lag in language development and concept formation as well.

It is extremely imperative that preschool children with special needs receive sensory and psychomotor stimulation, emphasizing the learning modes available to these children. The special needs child should be encouraged to become independent and active, rather than a passive receiver of the social and physical environment. Emphasis should be placed on the child's ability to communicate, especially if a child does not communicate in the usual fashion. It is particularly important for the special needs child to have contact with other children and not to be isolated from the world outside the family. With the recent trend of mainstreaming special needs children into the public schools, the opportunities for disabled and nondisabled children to interact are greatly increased.

The preschool child with a special need, like children at other stages of development, is impacted by a number of factors related to that need. Although the focus in this chapter is on physical special needs, there are factors related to physical disabilities that have a great impact on the child's social and emotional development as well.

First, the severity of the special need influences the child's attitude toward it. The better the special need can be camouflaged, the less difficulty the child will have developmentally.

Second, when the special need occurs will influence the child's development. If the special need occurred at birth, the child will have better adjustment than if it occurs later.

Third, the degree of restriction will greatly impact the child's development. The child who is blind or crippled, for example, will be more restricted than the child who is deaf or has a mild physical impairment.

Fourth, if others feel sorry for the child, this reaction may create feelings of martyrdom. If others are sympathetic and supportive, the child will develop a healthier attitude that should positively impact development.

Fifth, a child's attitude toward a special need will influence the effect it has on the child. Some children accept their special need, while many others will try to convince themselves they are not different from other children.

Sixth, the degree to which a child feels different from other children will affect the child's attitude toward the self. The more the child feels different from others, the greater the impact on development(3).

If the helping person is aware of factors such as those listed above, that person can greatly facilitate the child's emotional and social development. Even though many special needs children may not be able to do all of the activities other children do, the helping person should create a stimulating environment that will encourage these children to do those activities that they are capable of achieving.

Finally, Leo Buscaglia summarizes neatly the basic guidelines for those who work with children having special needs. He reminds us that children should be allowed to be their own person, unique and individual. That is, these children are people first, and that they have the same needs (love, self-actualization, and so on) and the same rights (even to fail) as other children. He suggests that it is the helping person's responsibility to listen, encourage, and facilitate the special needs child's growth by supplying guidance and other resources. We must allow these children to be themselves and to make choices about their lives without imposing our values, ideas, and attitudes on them(4).

Special Needs in Early
Childhood Literature

Recently there has been a veritable flood of books dealing with special needs for the middle school aged child and the adolescent--fiction books describing children with various handicaps as well as photodocumentaries about real children, many of them expressing a child's desire for acceptance and understanding as well as giving information about a specific handicap(5). The special needs preschooler can also benefit from a wide variety of literature dealing with that particular child's situation. Hopefully there will be a trend to add to the somewhat limited number of early-childhood books available on this topic.

According to Baskin and Harris, good literature for disabled children should:
1) Help them realize their affinity with the rest of humanity.
2) Help them deal with problems of all children, such as sibling rivalry.
3) Help them deal with their own special problems, including diminished functions, lessened independence, and restricted social opportunities.
4) Present alternative ways to react to situations so they can vicariously explore many possibilities.
5) Help them develop a realistic understanding of their limitations and potential(6).

In addition to these general characteristics of special needs literature, more specific criteria can be applied to literature selection depending on the particular special need of a child. Books for hearing impaired children should possess simple language, an easy to follow story line, and visual illustrations conveying action and meaning within the story. Visually disabled children need literature full of verbal details and vivid description; stories which address the emotions and involve the senses of touch, taste, and smell are especially useful. The child with a mobile disability has basically the same literature requirements of any preschool aged child, but can benefit from books which encourage socialization and show the child how to act in social situations(7). Literature is available dealing with the multi-handicapped child as well as the child who simply needs glasses or a hearing device.

Quality books about special needs children portray them as human beings, neither better nor worse than other children. The disability should be presented accurately and without pity. Ability rather than disability should be stressed. Special needs children must be presented as individuals who have successes and happy times as well as failures and sad times. All kinds of homes and family situations should be evident in story settings. Finally, disabled children must be shown solving their problems themselves, with appropriate help from others(8).

Responses to the literature. Although it is possible to locate books on specific disabilities to read to special needs children, these children have a need to be exposed to literature on all aspects of preschool development as well. In addition to facing their physical problems, special needs children are developing socially and emotionally and can benefit from the use of books on family relationships and peers, as well as literature on such topics as fears, anger, and so on. If a book concerning physical disabilities is read to a group including special needs children as well as those who are not disabled, special needs children who feel comfortable doing so can describe their disability to the others. In addition to discussion, the helping person can elicit other responses to the literature by activities such as:
1) Making a verbal or written list of things that are unique to each child in a group, stressing each person's positive attributes.
2) Using puppets to role play a situation with family or peers in a story.
3) Creating a book with words and illustrations, if possible, supplied by the child about accomplishments during the previous week or month.
4) Having the non-visually impaired child find magazine pictures representing various emotions all preschool children experience.
5) Painting or drawing of a favorite activity by the special needs child able to do so(9).

A special needs child often has a lag in social and emotional development, as well as a disability to face. This child may or may not have a high self-image(10). Much depends on how the adults in the child's life support and respond to the child. By hearing about and perhaps identifying with characters in the literature who also have special needs, the disabled child can greatly benefit. Not only can the special needs child discover that a disability is not so onerous that it cannot be mentioned in children's books, those who are not disabled can be helped to understand that their handicapped peers are children like themselves, sharing the same needs and pleasures and, above all, having the ability to do many things for themselves(11).

NOTES

1. Leo Buscaglia, The Disabled and Their Parents: A Counseling Challenge (Thorofare, New Jersey: Charles B. Slack, 1975), p. 11.
2. Linda Lucas and Marilyn Karrenbrock, The Disabled Child in the Library: Moving into the Mainstream (Littleton, Colorado: Libraries Unlimited, 1983), p. 108.
3. Elizabeth B. Hurlock, Child Development 6th ed. (New York: McGraw-Hill, 1978), pp. 124-125.
4. Buscaglia, pp. 20-21.
5. Zena Sutherland, Dianne Monson, and May Hill Arbuthnot, Children and Books 6th ed. (Glenview, Illinois: Scott, Foresman, and Company, 1981), p. 8.
6. Barbara Baskin and Karen Harris, The Exceptional Child in the School Library: Response and Strategy (Arlington, Virginia: ERIC Document, ED 097896, 1974).
7. Lucas and Karrenbrock, pp. 133-134.
8. Lucas and Karrenbrock, pp. 134-135.
9. Don Dinkmeyer, Developing Understanding of Self and Others (DUSO) Manual (Circle Pines, Minnesota: American Guidance Service, 1970); Lucas and Karrenbrock, The Disabled Child in the Library; Shirley C. Samuels, Enhancing Self-Concept in Early Childhood: Theory and Practice (New York: Human Sciences Press, 1977).
10. Samuels, p. 197.
11. Sutherland, Monson, and Arbuthnot, p. 8.

BOOKS

10.1 Allen, Marjorie. **One, Two, Three - AH-CHOO!** New York: Coward, McCann, and Geoghegan, 1980. 63 pp.

Young Wally is allergic to dust, fur, and feathers. Despite his allergy shots and medication, he is unable to keep a dog as a pet. Wally tries a frog and a snake as pets, but finally finds a hermit crab to be the perfect pet, especially when it wins a prize at a pet show.

IL: Ages 4-6

10.2 Brighton, Catherine. **My Hands, My World.** New York: Macmillan, 1984. 26 pp.

Maria, who is blind, says she must use her ears, hands, and nose to see the world. While her mother is busy working at home and her sister goes off to school, Maria spends time and shares secrets with her imaginary friend Bumper. When Maria's father returns from work, Maria can tell what kind of work he has done that day by the smell and feel of his clothing. Maria falls asleep smelling the powder from her bath and feeling her doll beside her.

IL: Ages 4-6

10.3 Brown, Tricia. **Someone Special, Just Like You.** New York: Holt, Rinehart, and Winston, 1984. 64 pp.

The limitations of young children with hearing and visual impairments and physical disabilities are mentioned, but more stress is placed on the many accomplishments these children are capable of. Along with their non-handicapped peers, the special children are shown participating in nursery school activities and doing things they enjoy.

IL: Ages 4-6

10.4 Cohen, Miriam. **See You Tomorrow, Charles.** New York: Greenwillow Books, 1983. 28 pp.

Some classmates give Charles, a blind boy, special treatment and are embarrassed if anyone mentions words such as "seeing" or "look" around him. The children discuss the things Charles can do well and everyone enjoys a story he tells the class about Superman. On the playground, Charles and two of his classmates wander through an open door and get locked in a dark basement. The other two children are frightened, but Charles feels along the wall to find the door and enables them all to get out of the basement.

IL: Ages 4-6

10.5 Cohen. **So What?** see Ch. 8.

10.6 Corrigan, Kathy. **Emily Umily.** Toronto: Annick Press, 1984. 24 pp.

Five year old Emily doesn't enjoy speaking in front of her kindergarten class because she has the habit of saying "um" quite frequently. The rest of her class laugh at her when she speaks, calling her Umily, and soon Emily hates kindergarten and becomes withdrawn. Only when she accompanies her mother to a yoga class does Emily discover the use of "um" in meditation. She happily demonstrates for her kindergarten class the following day.

IL: Ages 4-6

10.7 Greenfield, Eloise. **Darlene.** New York: Methuen, 1980. 29 pp.

Six year old Darlene, who is confined to a wheelchair, resents having to spend the day with her uncle and cousin Joanne. The two girls play board games and play catch with a ball while Darlene impatiently waits for her mother's return. Then Darlene and Joanne play an adapted version of jump rope and later join Darlene's uncle in singing. By the time her mother returns, Darlene is having so much fun she wants to stay.

IL: Ages 4-6

10.8 Keller, Holly. **Cromwell's Glasses.** New York: Greenwillow Books, 1982. 28 pp.

Cromwell the rabbit is nearsighted and has complications because of it--he frequently stumbles, has difficulties playing games, can't help out much at home, etc. Once Cromwell has an eye examination and is fitted for glasses, he is thrilled with his better eyesight but his siblings and friends poke fun at him and call him names. When an older sister helps Cromwell demonstrate how much better he can see to play at the playground, however, the other rabbits accept him with his new glasses.

IL: Ages 4-6

10.9 Rabe, Berniece. **The Balancing Girl.** New York: E.P. Dutton, 1981. 28 pp.

Margaret is very good at balancing objects while in her wheelchair or on her crutches. A boy in her class, Tommy, belittles Margaret's efforts and even knocks down a castle Margaret makes out of classroom objects. When Margaret devises an idea for a domino chain for the school carnival, her class enthusiastically helps out. Margaret is responsible for raising the most money at her school and even Tommy is anxious to buy a chance at setting the domino chain in motion.

IL: Ages 4-6

10.10 Rosenberg, Maxine. **My Friend Leslie: The Story of a Handicapped Child.** New York: Lothrop, Lee, and Shepard, 1983. 42 pp.

A kindergarten girl tells of her friendship with Leslie, a multi-handicapped child who has been mainstreamed into a public school classroom. Although Leslie wears two hearing aids, has a visual impairment, and also has mobility problems, she is an outstanding reader and participates in many activities. Leslie is well accepted by her classmates who are eager to do things for her, but her friend explains that Leslie doesn't need help most of the time.

IL: Ages 4-6

10.11 Sargent, Susan and Donna Wirt. **My Favorite Place.** Nashville: Abingdon, 1983. 27 pp.

A young blind girl accompanies her parents on a trip to the beach. She and her mother wade in the ocean, while her father gets out the picnic lunch. Later the three of them run along the beach trying to avoid the waves. The little girl tells why she loves the beach--it is the only place where she can hear, smell, taste, and touch all the things she likes best.

IL: Ages 4-6

10.12 Snell, Nigel. **Peter Gets a Hearing Aid.** London: Hamish Hamilton, 1980. 27 pp.

Although he doesn't always mind when he's being reprimanded, Peter finds it difficult to hear his mother and teacher. He also speaks differently from the other children at his school. When his mother takes Peter for a hearing test, a friendly doctor examines him and Peter participates in some fun tests. Peter is fitted for a new hearing aid and is surprised and happy with the results.

IL: Ages 4-6

10.13 Tusa, Tricia. **Libby's New Glasses.** New York: Holiday House, 1984. 28 pp.

Unhappy with the way she looks in her new eyeglasses, Libby packs a bag and runs away from home. She spots an ostrich with its head in the sand that claims it is too embarrassed to show its face. Libby lists the ostrich's virtues to make it feel better and is surprised to see when the ostrich lifts its head, it wears eyeglasses also. The two take a walk and are so impressed with how clearly things look that they decide wearing glasses isn't so bad after all.

IL: Ages 4-6

10.14 Wahl, Jan. **Button Eye's Orange.** New York: Frederick Warne, 1980. 42 pp.

Button Eye, a cloth dog with a leg sewn on backward, loves his owner, a small boy who wears a leg brace. Upon hearing the boy's wish for an orange, Button Eye searches a marketplace for one and must fend off a rat and fruits and vegetables which come to life. Making it only part way home, Button Eye collapses on the sidewalk with his orange. Encouraged to seek out his lost toy, the boy walks farther with his leg brace on than ever before and finds Button Eye.

IL: Ages 4-6

Author Index

Includes authors and joint authors.
Numbers refer to individual entry number.

Title Index

Numbers refer to individual entry number

Subject Index

Numbers refer to individual entry number.

ABOUT THE COMPILERS

JEAN A. PARDECK is a Reading Specialist in private practice. She has published in such journals as **Child Welfare, Social Work in Education,** and **The School Counselor.** Jean received her M.Ed. in Reading from the University of Nebraska-Lincoln.

JOHN T. PARDECK, the Director of the Social Work Program at Arkansas State University, is a member of the Academy of Certified Social Workers. He has published in such journals as **Social Work, Child Welfare, Social Work in Education,** and **The School Counselor.** Dr. Pardeck is a member of the Editorial Board of the journal **Early Child Development and Care.** John received his Ph.D. in Social Work from Saint Louis University School of Social Service.